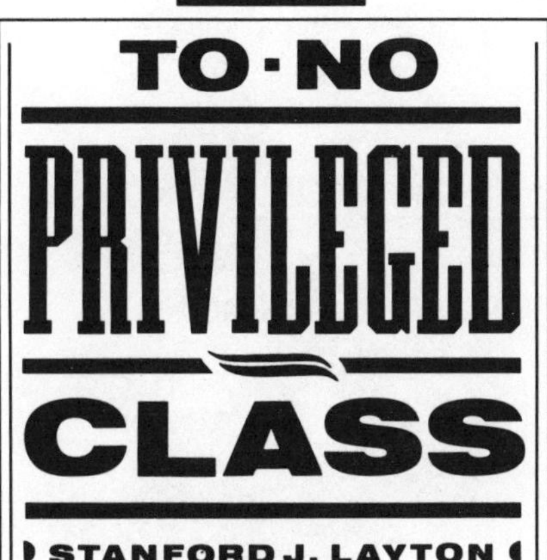

TO·NO PRIVILEGED CLASS

STANFORD J. LAYTON

Charles Redd Monographs in Western History No.17

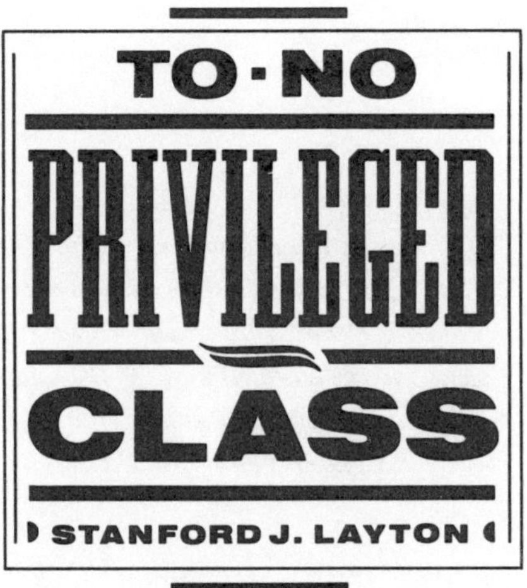

THE RATIONALIZATION OF HOMESTEADING AND RURAL LIFE IN THE EARLY TWENTIETH-CENTURY AMERICAN WEST

Brigham Young University
Charles Redd Center for Western Studies

The Charles Redd Monographs in Western History are made possible by a grant from Charles Redd. This grant served as the basis for the establishment of the Charles Redd Center for Western Studies at Brigham Young University.

———

Center editor: Thomas G. Alexander
Press editor: Howard A. Christy

Library of Congress Cataloging-in-Publication Data

Layton, Stanford J., 1941–
    To no privileged class.
    (Charles Redd monographs in western history; no. 17)
    Includes index.
    1. Homestead law—Economic aspects—West (U.S.)—History.
2. Homestead law—Social aspects—West (U.S.)—History. 3.
Frontier and pioneer life—West (U.S.)—History. 4. Public
lands—West (U.S.)—History.
    I. Title. II. Series.
    HD1339.U5L39 1987   331.1'6'0978   87-14299
    ISBN 0-941214-59-1

Distributed by Signature Books, 350 S. 400 E., Suite G4, Salt
Lake City, Utah 84111

Table of
Contents

Introduction

The history of the origin and supersession of the enlarged homestead acts of the early twentieth-century American West is particularly instructive to the modern student of public resource policy in the United States. It reveals the profundity, timelessness, and complexity of the basic resource management questions that are being debated today. Indeed, the ownership, management, and use of public lands is one of the most enduring domestic issues of the twentieth century and is certain to continue into the twenty-first century and beyond.

Much has been published about the various twentieth-century homestead acts. They were, according to the leading authorities on public land history in America, ill-advised in concept and detrimental in fact. This is particularly so with the Enlarged Homestead Act, also known as the Dry Farm Homestead Act, of February 1909, and the Stock Raising Homestead Act, also known as the Grazing Homestead Act, of December 1916. Benjamin Hibbard, in his brief discussion of these two acts, describes them as impractical and judges that "they have fallen far short of expectations."[1] Everett Dick, referring to the reduced residency requirement of the Enlarged Homestead Act, paraphrases Walter Prescott Webb's witticism that it was a humanitarian gesture to recognize that "the point of starvation would be reached before the culmination of the [five-year] required residence."[2] E. Louise Peffer has rendered the most vigorous criticism of these two homestead acts, analyzing them as not only deceitful (inviting the unsuspecting homesteader to certain failure) but also as responsible for the rise in farm tenancy. Further, she asserts that these two enlarged homestead measures were patently antagonistic to the basic principles of conservation.[3] And the foremost authority on the subject, Paul W. Gates, has labeled these acts simply as "unwise."[4]

This study represents no challenge to the view that these homestead acts bore much bitter fruit. It is revisionist only in that it appeals for a clarification of the national circumstances surrounding the enactment of these measures—how Congress and two presidents were persuaded to initiate this legislation that has since been condemned so heartily by historians. In view of the far-reaching social, political, demographic, and economic ramifications of these acts—hundreds of thousands of Americans were affected directly and millions indirectly—the issue warrants this further examination.

Neither Hibbard nor Dick specifically addresses the question of how the Enlarged Homestead Act and Stock Raising Homestead Act took shape and gained passage. Peffer, on the other hand, is not only specific, she is emphatic: the acts were contrived and manipulated through Congress by the "militant" West, united and brash in its determination to exploit the public domain for its own particular ends. Gates identifies several of the prime movers behind these acts as westerners, but he acknowledges that "the West did not put up a united front" in support of the Stock Raising Homestead Act, and in a number of other ways he stops far short of Peffer in his conclusions.

Although past research offers conflicting explanations for passage of the acts, the reader should come to understand from the analysis that follows that the issue of public land cession in the early twentieth century was neither sectional nor partisan. It was, in fact, only partially political. Any historical inquiry into the origin of the Enlarged Homestead Act and the Stock Raising Homestead Act must scan the political arena but cannot afford to stop there. These measures were inextricably tied to the great social issues of the day, to demographic and economic shifts, and to a certain rhetorical binge about the virtues of life on the land as the American public struggled to adjust to the closing of a three-hundred-year-old frontier. The period of adjustment lasted a full generation, finally reaching its conclusion in the Taylor Grazing Act of 1934. A look at that momentous development reveals that the demise of the twentieth-century homestead acts, like their derivation, was hardly sectional in nature.

The Enlarged Homestead Act and Stock Raising Homestead Act were the last two of four homestead acts passed during the Progressive Era. They were preceded by the Kinkaid Act of 1904 and the Forest Homestead Act of 1906. With these several acts the Progressive Era witnessed the culmination of the homesteading urge in America, an urge that was to outrun the resources of the nation and was therefore to flounder on the rocks of actual experience. But only in a general way does this study deal with the degree of success or failure experienced by the dry farming and grazing homesteaders, a topic well covered by Gates. It is certain that these experiments in public land disposal met neither the expectations of their reform-minded sponsors nor the promise of the back-to-the-land writers. But to question the historical validity of these enlarged homestead acts is to focus on an essentially meaningless point. Much more significant is a reconstruction of the matrix from which they emerged and in which they operated. With a concept of the relationships between the ideas that spawned these acts and the reality of conditions then existing in the nation, the reader may be better able to gauge present and future courses of action as similar issues continue to arise.

CHAPTER ONE

The Country-Life Movement

To understand the origins of enlarged homesteading in the early twentieth-century American West, the student of history must first look to the East and the country-life movement of the Progressive Era. This movement, short-lived and poorly understood, is easily traced to Theodore Roosevelt. Whether or not the idea came from the president himself is not of great significance as a historical question. What is significant is that Roosevelt at least provided form and substance by creating the Commission on Country Life in 1908 and by naming Liberty Hyde Bailey as its chairman.

Roosevelt himself defined the country-life "problem" in his introduction to the commission's report issued in 1910. "The farmer has not received the attention that the city worker has received and has not been able to express himself as the city worker has done," he said. This has had unfortunate consequences for the entire nation, he continued, since, despite the great growth of the industrial sector, the well-being of the commonwealth depends upon the well-being of the farmer. Therefore, "the strengthening of country life is the strengthening of the whole nation."[1]

In many ways this was typical of Theodore Roosevelt. His experience as a cattleman in the Badlands during the early 1880s is well known,[2] and it is certain that his identification with and compassion for the rural sector of American society ran deep throughout his adult life. Predictably, Roosevelt was quick to adopt the suggestion from his chief forester and fellow Progressive, Gifford Pinchot, to appoint a commission "as a means for directing the attention of the Nation to the problems of the farm, and for securing the necessary knowledge of the actual conditions of life in the open country."[3] The president had on several occasions conferred with the old Populist, Tom Watson, and the eminent leader of the farmers' cooperative movement in Ireland, Sir Horace Plunkett, on the subject of improving living conditions for farm people. He had, in fact, asked Plunkett to confer with Pinchot on the matter, and it was out of that conference that Pinchot's suggestion originated.[4]

In the person of Liberty Hyde Bailey, the president found exactly the right man to chair the new commission. Born into a Michigan farm family in the spring of 1848, Bailey grew to maturity on that farm and developed an enduring attachment to the soil. He enrolled at Michigan Agricultural College, earning his bachelor's degree in 1882 and his master's degree in 1886. For three years, beginning in 1885, he served on the faculty of his alma mater as a professor of horticulture and landscape gardening. In 1882 he joined the Cornell University faculty as a professor of horticulture; by 1903 he had risen to the position of dean of the College of Agriculture. A man of great energy and ambition, Bailey somehow found the time to complete the requirements for a law degree from the University of Wisconsin in 1907. A dozen years later, at the age of sixty-one, he completed a doctorate in literature from the University of Vermont.

During his lengthy career as student, professor, and dean, L. H. Bailey authored dozens of texts, manuals, and monographs on the subject of horticulture and agriculture. He also established a reputation as an editor, especially in the production of three multivolume cyclopedias on farming and gardening. He held honorary memberships in a number of horticultural societies, including the Royal Society of London, which awarded him the Vietchian Medal in 1898.

These accomplishments and distinctions notwithstanding, it is doubtful that L. H. Bailey's name would be well remembered today were it not for his involvement in the country-life movement. Following his appointment as chairman on the Commission on Country Life, Bailey dedicated himself to the work at hand with the same commitment that had characterized his work as a scientist. In a half-dozen books, dozens of articles, and an indeterminate number of public addresses, he outlined and refined the assumptions behind the movement, identified the problems and proposed a number of ways to approach the solutions, and publicized the movement with grace and dignity. It may be too much to say he was the father of the country-life movement, but in the fullest sense he was its acknowledged leader and most articulate spokesman.

Also appointed to the Country Life Commission were Kenyon L. Butterfield, Gifford Pinchot, Walter Hines Page, Charles S. Barrett, Henry Wallace, and William A. Beard. In terms of credentials Roosevelt chose well. Butterfield's background was similar to Bailey's. He was born in Michigan and held degrees from Michigan Agricultural College and the

University of Michigan. He, too, earned a law degree, taking it from Amherst College in 1910. After three years as president of Rhode Island State College, he returned to Michigan Agricultural College in 1906 as president. He published four books between 1908 and 1923, each dealing with conditions in rural America. In so doing he joined Bailey as an acknowledged spokesman of the country-life movement.

Gifford Pinchot was born in Connecticut of immigrant parents and received his early education in private schools. He graduated from Yale in 1889 and then went to Europe to continue his study of forestry. In 1903 he accepted a professorship in that science at Yale. By the time of his appointment to the Country Life Commission he had been chief of the U.S. Forest Service for a decade.

Walter Hines Page, a New Yorker, had a well-established reputation as an editor at the time of his appointment to the commission. In addition to having spent twelve years on the staff of the *New York Forum*, he had also served as editor of *Atlantic Monthly* for two years and was a partner in Doubleday, Page & Company, publishers. It was he who created *World's Work* in 1900, a periodical he edited for the next thirteen years. Charles S. Barrett, born and raised on a Georgia farm, was well known by 1908 for his activity in the organization of farmers. When appointed to the Country Life Commission he had already begun his lengthy tenure as president of the highly influential National Farmers' Union.

Henry Wallace represented the first of three distinguished generations of Henry Wallaces from Iowa. He founded, owned, and edited *Wallaces' Farm and Dairy* (later called *Wallaces' Farmer*) and authored such books as *Uncle Henry's Letters to the Farm Boy* and *Letters to the Farm Folks*. William A. Beard, of Sacramento, California, enjoyed a solid reputation as a journalist and student of public affairs on the basis of his work with the *Great Western Magazine*.

The problem before the commission was "to state, with some fullness of detail, the present conditions of country life, to point out the causes that may have led to its present lack of organization, to suggest methods by which it may be redirected, the drift to the city arrested, the natural rights of the farmer maintained, and an organized rural life developed that will promote the prosperity of the whole nation."[5] Toward that end the commission proved remarkably efficient. Hosting thirty public hearings attended by rural people from forty states and assimilating 120,000 answers to printed questionnaires sent to farm families across the nation, the commission organized its findings and presented them to the president in a 150-page report on January 23, 1909. It completed these tasks in less than six months. The key findings are mentioned here not only for what they disclose about the economic and social milieu within which the Enlarged Homestead Act and Stock Raising Homestead Act had their origins, but they are mentioned as well for what they disclose about the attitudes held by a highly touted group of eastern Progressives toward the agrarian sector of America at the end of the first decade of the twentieth century. Five of the seven commissioners were from the East. At least four of them—Pinchot, Bailey, Butterfield, and Page—are identifiable as Progressives.[6]

Measured by historical standards, the report disclosed, the American farmer had shown steady progress in his quest for economic and social betterment. Measured by contemporary standards shared by the urban community, however, the nation's farmers were disadvantaged and depressed. According to the report, "agriculture is not commercially as profitable as it is entitled to be for the labor and energy that the farmer expends and the risks that he assumes, and . . . the social conditions in the open country are far short of their possibilities."[7] There were a number of factors bearing on this unfortunate state of affairs. Among them were an inexact knowledge among the farmers of the farming conditions and possibilities within their regions, inadequate public schools in rural areas, poor highways, continuous soil erosion, absence of an equitable farm-loan system, shortage of farm labor, the arduous and unrewarding life faced by farm women, and the lack of adequate public health supervision. But the greatest problem, the one that had to be resolved before any of the others could be addressed, was that of systematic exploitation of the farmers by "the interests"—large, unregulated monopolies.

The Country Life Commission proposed solutions to each of these problems, placing responsibility on the federal government to solve many of the problems while advising that state and local governments, voluntary organizations, and even individual initiative could solve others. Of primary importance in solving "the whole problem of ultimate permanent reconstruction" of rural America was the launching of three great programs: (1) a comprehensive survey of the resources and conditions upon which farming was based in any particular region; (2) a full-blown system of extension work in which specialists would communicate and work directly with farmers and farmers' wives in the promotion of better farming, better sanitation, better homemaking, and all other aspects of country living; and (3) a campaign for rural progress that would unite teachers, doctors, editors, clergymen, and other professionals in a concerted effort to enhance the comforts and security of life in the country.

In their discussion of solutions, as with their delineation of the problems, the members of the Country Life Commission devoted a good deal of attention to the exploitation of the farmers by the organized interests. Nothing betrays the Progressive bent of the commission's report more implicitly than this emphasis. For example, in lamenting the speculative holding of large tracts of land by certain individuals, the commission urged that the federal government take all necessary precautions to guarantee that all future reclamation projects "proceed under conditions insuring their subdivision into small farm units and their settlement by men who would both own them and till them." Noting the rapid trend toward monopolistic control of rivers by large utility companies, the commission recommended an end to perpetual grants of water power privileges. They urged that monopolistic control of streams valuable for irrigation be discouraged since "the ownership of water for irrigation is no less important than the ownership of land." They recommended that forest reserves be created on watersheds, thereby ending the theretofore common practice of private exploitation of timberlands with its attendant menace to topsoil conservation of the farmlands below. Finally, the commission advised the Interstate Commerce Commission to continue an aggressive policy aimed at eliminating the many flagrant abuses perpetrated by the railroads at the expense of the farmer. In a nutshell, the commission concluded:

> We find that there is need of a new general attitude toward legislation, in the way of safeguarding the farmers' natural rights and interests. It is natural that the organized and consolidated interests should be strongly in mind in the making of legislation. We recommend that the welfare of the farmer and countryman be also kept in mind in the construction of laws. We especially recommend that his interests be considered and safeguarded in any new legislation on the tariff, on regulation on railroads, control or regulating of corporations and of speculation, river, swamp, and forest legislation, and public health regulation.[8]

It was obviously a deep conviction of the members of the Country Life Commission that once the farmers were protected from "the interests," the other problems attending farm life could be solved. This, of course, was a primary end toward which the study was commissioned: proposing the means necessary to make farm life attractive enough to slow the flow of farmers, and particularly farm youth, to the cities. The major premise of the Country Life Commission study was that farming was a dignified and virtuous way of making a living and that ordinarily it was the environment best suited to the raising of responsible and well-adjusted children. In the opening paragraph of its report, the Country Life Commission observed that "not only in the material wealth that they produce, but in the supply of independent and strong citizenship, the agricultural people constitute the very foundation of our national efficiency." In the conclusion of its introductory section, the commission referred to the necessity of preserving "a race of men in the open country that, in the future as in the past, will be the stay and strength of the nation in time of war and its guiding and controlling spirit in time of peace." The farmer has inherited a strong tradition of individualism and has learned to carry his own weight, the commission noted further. "The city exploits the country: the country does not exploit the city," was the corollary.

By expressing these sentiments on the virtues of the yeoman farmer, the commission members were marching in rhetorical cadence with Theodore Roosevelt. In his letter of commission to Professor Bailey, the president opened by asserting: "No nation has ever achieved permanent greatness unless this greatness was based on the well-being of the great farmer class, the men who live on the soil; for it is upon their welfare, material and moral, that the welfare of the rest of the nation ultimately rests."[9] As if that were not explicit enough, he also included an excerpt from an address he had given a year earlier in commemoration of the fiftieth anniversary of the nation's first agricultural colleges.

> There is but one person whose welfare is as vital to the welfare of the whole country as is that of the wage-worker who does manual labor, and that is the tiller of the soil—the farmer. If there is one lesson taught by history, it is that the permanent greatness of any State must ultimately depend more upon the character of its country population than upon anything else. No growth of cities, no growth of wealth can make up for loss in either the number or the character of the farming population.[10]

By reflecting the traditional Progressive antipathy to monopolistic practices, which the members of the commission saw as a rapidly developing trend within the agricultural sector, the report contained a number of specific recommendations indirectly in favor of a liberalized homesteading policy. But even more significant, the Country Life Commission represented the beginning of the entire country-life movement, which slowly transformed into the back-to-the-land movement; and the back-to-the-land movement figured *directly* in the liberalization of national homesteading policy. Because of its central importance to the story at hand, that transformation is worth a closer look.

The most completely developed treatment of the country-life movement was offered by L. H. Bailey in his book appropriately titled *The Country Life Movement in the United States*. He defined the movement as a desire not only to improve farming but also to improve the quality of farm life, a desire "to make country life what it is capable of becoming."[11] For this purpose it was essential to recognize agriculture not merely as an occupation but as a civilization. The task at hand was to reestablish that civilization as one attractive enough to keep intelligent, aspiring, and progressive people within it. Anticipating a certain illegitimate exploitation of the movement, Bailey nevertheless considered it sound at the center and foresaw momentous undercurrents within it.

> For the next twenty-five years we may expect it to have great influence on the course of events, for it will require this length of time to balance up society. Demagogues and fakirs will take advantage of it for personal gain. Tradesmen will make much of it. Writers are even now beginning to sensationalize it.
>
> But there will also arise countrymen with statesmanship in them; if not so, then we cannot make the progress that we need. The movement will have its significant political aspect, and we may look for governors of states and perhaps more than one President of the United States to come out of it.[12]

Although Bailey was overly sanguine in his prediction of the political effects of the movement, he was certainly justified in his belief that it was the start of something big. And even as he wrote, in 1911, he betrayed a suspicion that the country-life movement was being misunderstood, that it was being mistaken for an appeal to the urbanite to relocate in the country. He referred to the "present popular back-to-the-land agitation" as an urban impulse stemming from the desire of city dwellers to escape from congested areas, an impulse abetted by dubious propaganda from opportunistic realtors. He viewed any exodus from the cities to the farms as an awful perversion of the country-life movement, and he cautioned strongly against it. "The country-life movement and back-to-the-land movements are not only little related, but in many ways they are distinctly antagonistic."[13]

But Bailey did not conceal his opinion that most city people would find a better life in the country. This was, in fact, one of his most deeply held convictions. What he argued, rather, was that such a demographic shift would be bad for the country. The distinction is an important one, for it underscores the basic dilemma of Bailey's position: how to convey the belief that farming was potentially, if not actually, the most desirable of all possible livelihoods without encouraging, at the same time, the incipient back-to-the-land movement. His argument that the nation needed better farmers, not more farmers, was never quite as stimulating or persuasive as his argument that the cities were insufferable in comparison to farms. On the latter point he minced no words.

> The fundamental weakness in our civilization is the fact that the city and the country represent antagonistic forces. Sympathetically, they have been and are opposed. The city lives on the country. It always tends to destroy its province. The city sits like a parasite, running out its roots into the open country and draining it of its substance. The city takes everything to itself—materials, money, men—and gives back only what it does not want; it does not reconstruct or even maintain its contributory country. Many country places are already sucked dry.[14]

Conversely, the farmer is "the natural balance-force or the middle-wheel of society," the steady and conservative force lying between the laborers on the one hand and the syndicated interests on the other. As such, he is the controlling element in society to a much greater extent than commonly recognized. Further, unlike the city dweller, every farmer has the opportunity of founding a dynasty. "City properties," Bailey wrote, "may come and go, rented houses may be removed, stocks and bonds may rise and fall, but the land still remains; and a man can remain on the land and subsist with it so long as he knows how to handle it properly."[15]

Much of what Bailey said was reiterated in slightly modified terms by his colleague, Kenyon L. Butterfield, whose most explicit analysis, *The Farmer and the New Day,* was published eight years after Bailey's *Country Life Movement.* By then the country-life movement was in atrophy, but Butterfield did not acknowledge that fact. As much as Bailey, he was of the belief that the independence of the yeoman must be preserved above all, that "true democracy requires that the man who tills the land shall control the land he tills."[16] He too saw country life, particularly a revitalized country life, as being distinctly preferable to city life. In fact, his praise of farmers bordered on the prodigal.

> American farm life has bred the most skillful farmers, the most intelligent rural citizens, the most engaging farm homes to be found anywhere in the world. This praise applies to the real American farmer, the owner and active manager of a family-size farm, who came of the best blood of pioneer America, whose intelligence is comparable with that of the leading groups of citizens of the Republic, many of whose sons and daughters have made their way into recognized leadership in business, industry, and the professions. It is difficult to speak with restraint of this man or his achievements. He conquered a huge continent of rich soil for civilization. He carried to the frontier an eager desire for education, the democratic impulse, and the fear of the Lord. He has helped fight his country's battles. He has been the bedrock of representative government.[17]

Bailey and Butterfield were the purists among the country-life thinkers and writers, and in their subsequent writings they adhered closely to the basic tenets laid down by the Country Life Commission. These tenets may be recapitulated briefly as follows: The rural element in American society had been, and continued to be, the most essential of all elements in the establishment and preservation of a strong, stable, and democratic America. Because of this it was necessary to curb the recent and alarming rush of rural Americans to the cities. In order to do this, government must join with farmers and various professions in revitalizing conditions in the country such that rural people would no longer need to move to the cities to fill certain voids in their lives. The object was to keep rural people in the country rather than encouraging urban people to migrate to the country. Some interchange of populations was fine, even desirable; but a heavy interchange was unhealthy. Many urbanites, it appeared, were scurrying to the farms without the knowledge, skill, or capital to be successful as farmers. Not only were they in a poor position to make a contribution to rural America (and, therefore, to America as a whole), but they ran the risk of ruining their own lives as well.

To the chagrin of Bailey and Butterfield, the country-life tenets were poorly observed by a number of other writers. To survey these other writings is to see, step by step, how the distinction between the country-life movement and the back-to-the-land movement became blurred and how the former came to degenerate into the latter. There were many such writers, but only three need to be discussed here in order to illustrate the direction the country-life movement took during the second decade of the twentieth century.

In a series of articles published in the Progressive-oriented *Outlook* in 1910, Sir Horace Plunkett advanced several suggestions he thought would promote the tangible achievements of the country-life movement. He hoped to "be able to show that this is not one of those new movements by which nothing but resolutions are moved."[18] Using the same style of piquant narrative throughout these articles, he advanced the thesis that the key to a successful upgrading of country life lay in effective organization among the farmers. It was, of course, Plunkett's success at organizing farmers in Ireland that had won him an international reputation and had brought him to the attention of Theodore Roosevelt. But Plunkett held a firsthand familiarity with conditions in America as well as in Ireland, having a decade of experience as a rancher at the base of the Rockies.

Sir Horace was not perceptibly less reserved than either Bailey or Butterfield in his testimony to the virtues of the yeoman farmer. Subscribing to the Aristotelian dictum that "where husbandmen and men of small fortune predominate, government will be guided by law,"[19] he foresaw as inevitable the consequences of continuing urban expansion:

> The country is thus the reservoir from which the town draws its best citizenship. You cannot keep on indefinitely skimming the pan and have equally good milk left. In America the drain may continue a while longer without the inevitable consequences becoming plainly visible; but sooner or later, if the balance of trade in this human traffic be not adjusted, the raw material out of which urban society is made will be seriously deteriorated. When that time comes, the symptoms of National degeneracy will be properly charged against those who failed to foresee the evil and treat the cause.[20]

For this reason Plunkett was deeply concerned over the rapidly shrinking number of rural Americans. Like Bailey and Butterfield, he was aware of the nascent back-to-the-land movement in the opposite direction; but unlike them he was not apprehensive that this represented a movement of the *wrong* people to the country. Rather, he was worried that an insufficient number of people—any people—would be there to take up the slack in rural areas. "To my bucolic intelligence," he penned in his sparkling style, "it would seem that against the 'back to the land' movement of Saturday afternoon the captious critic might set the rural exodus of Monday morning."[21]

Many of the views on the country-life movement expressed before 1912, including those of Plunkett, were included in a textbook by G. Walter Fiske entitled *The Challenge of the Country: A Study of Country Life Opportunity*. It was written at the request of the International Committee of Young Men's Christian Associations. Not surprisingly, it reflected a strong spiritual emphasis in its approach to the country-life problem. Generally anchored to the basic tenets established by Bailey and Butterfield, *The Challenge of the Country* lacked the subtleties and discipline that characterized the works of these primary writers. It tended toward dogmatism and stridency in its condemnation of city life and its elocution of country life. Its tendentious nature foreshadowed a leading feature of the back-to-the-land genre of literature.

Exemplary of Fiske's style and tone is his reference to the city as the "graveyard of the national physique," and his continuation of that point in the following vein:

> With its moral and industrial overstrain, it [the city] is the burial place of health, as well as youthful ambitions and hopes, for many a young person not accustomed to its high-geared life. The nervous system rebels against the city pace. In an incognito life the character crumbles under the subtle disintegration of city temptations.[22]

The city sapped the strength and virtue of those who ventured within it, giving nothing in return. It was wholly dependent on the folly of people for its existence. For centuries country people had made their way without cities. They could do so again. The cities, on the other hand, could not survive a month without sustenance from the country. The dogmatism of Fiske is particularly apparent in his discussion of the virtues of rural life. Revealing of the entire format of the book is the insertion, early in chapter 2, of "The Country Boy's Creed":

> I believe that the country which God made is more beautiful than the city which man made; that life out-of-doors and in touch with the earth is the natural life of man. I believe that work is work wherever I find it; but that work with Nature is more inspiring than work with the most intricate machinery. I believe that the dignity of labor depends not on what you do, but on how you do it; that opportunity comes to a boy on the farm as often as to a boy in the city; that life is larger and freer and happier on the farm than in the town; that my success depends not upon my location, but upon myself,—not upon my dreams, but upon what I actually do, not upon luck but upon pluck. I believe in working

when you work and playing when you play, and in giving and demand-
ing a square deal in every act of life.[23]

The book ends with a similar credo entitled "The Productive Life
Fellowship" by Thomas Nixon Carver.

Another important country-life thinker was Lyman Beecher Stowe,
who presented his views in two articles produced for *Outlook* in 1912.
Addressing himself to the question of population shifts, Stowe noted the
acceleration in the city-to-country movement and expressed some concern
that it could reach an undesirable dimension. For the time being, at least,
the migration from the farms to the cities was still far from being bal-
anced, and the flow of urbanites to the country "should be stimulated in
every legitimate way."[24] True to the basic tenets of the country-life movement, however, Stowe cautioned strongly against hasty removals to the
country. Only those city people who had gained some previous experience
in farming should contemplate a move to the farms. Otherwise, heartbreak and failure would likely await them.

Continuing this theme, Stowe argued that, once equipped with farm
experience, city-bred youths who desired to farm were likely to become
better farmers than their country counterparts. Perhaps, on this point, he
did not depart widely from Bailey and Butterfield in their basic assumptions, but he certainly took the point well beyond anything they would
have considered comfortable. Superficially, at least, his case seemed logical. The city lads usually held the advantage of better schooling, gaining
therefrom a wider range of skills to aid them in managing the "business"
of a farm. Beginning their practical knowledge of farming with a clean
slate, they had nothing to "unlearn." Further, by personally seeking a
livelihood from the farm, the city boys were less apt to regard that type of
work as drudgery than were the farm youths who had never known another
life.[25]

Closely related to this theme, and perhaps of greater importance in
assigning historical significance to Stowe's work, was his explicit conten-
tion that farm life was likely to be of tremendous therapeutic value to
many city misfits, particularly juvenile delinquents. This was a sharp
departure from Bailey and Butterfield, and it represented a key transi-
tional link between country-life and back-to-the-land literature. Stowe
recounted, for example, the amazing success story of the State Agricultural and Industrial School of New York, to which lawbreaking juveniles
were sentenced. Seven years prior, the prison walls had been razed and

military discipline jettisoned in favor of a huge communal farming complex. The young inmates responded to the new format with great enthusiasm, priding themselves on the production of prize crops and livestock, hosting their own fairs, experimenting with the latest scientific techniques, and even, on occasion, preparing and reading papers on new agricultural procedures to their assembled colleagues. Rehabilitation was remarkable, Stowe claimed. More than a third of the discharged delinquents had found gainful employment on farms, and many of them were making fine progress toward gaining ownership of their own farms. In addition, more than a hundred parolees were holding jobs on farms. This was not an isolated case. Similar experiments, with similar results, were also observable at the Lincoln Agricultural School, for homeless boys, in Lincolndale, New York, and at the National Farm School, for Jewish lads from city ghettos, near Philadelphia. Still other examples were the Baron DeHirsch Agricultural School at Woodbine, New Jersey, and the Billings Polytechnic Institute in Montana.[26]

Nor did this tell the entire story, according to Stowe. Farm life also worked its extraordinary therapy on the sick and debilitated. A prominent New York physician, upon examining two "pale, nervous, overwrought and anemic" teenage boys, advised their father that if he wanted his family to be perpetuated he had only one alternative: to buy a farm, put the boys on it, and keep them there.[27] The author did not dwell on this point, but in mentioning it he gave the back-to-the-land writers an important cue.

Whatever his credibility, it is indisputable that Lyman Beecher Stowe expressed himself with a literary skill and finesse rare among the subsequent writers on the theme of country therapy. Illustrative of his style is the exciting generalization with which he concluded his second article:

> Just as Hercules's opponent Antaeus doubled his strength every time he touched mother earth, so the men of the cities renew their strength when they return to the land. Likewise exhausted lands are renewed by the scientific agricultural methods of the city-bred and country-trained farmer. In short, the bringing together of exhausted city men and exhausted county lands means the renewal of both.[28]

Within a short time, then, strange things had begun to happen to the original country-life movement as conceived in the Roosevelt-Pinchot alembic, brought to life by their specially appointed commission, and given an intellectual polish by L. H. Bailey. According to the original precepts of the movement, the agricultural sector of American society was no longer receiving those social, cultural, and economic dividends to which it was entitled. Consequently, an alarming migration from farm to city was in process, particularly among the younger generation. If this demographic trend were not arrested, a qualitative degradation of the entire nation would surely result, since the country continued to be, as it had been traditionally, the mainstay of a productive and virtuous America. In order to arrest this trend, country life must be revitalized and upgraded in all aspects such that its attractiveness to its native sons would exceed that of the cities. While the cooperation of many agencies would be required toward this end, the lead would have to be taken by the federal government.

Almost immediately these precepts were subjected to a variety of special emphases by other students of the country-life movement. Sir Horace Plunkett suggested that migration to the city did not necessarily have to be arrested; stimulating a flow of city people to the country could balance the loss. This suggestion was taken a step further by Lyman Beecher Stowe, who argued that an exodus from the country in tandem with a movement of trained city people to the country was in fact the key to solving the entire country-life problem. G. Walter Fiske, whose textbook may have reached a wider audience than any other source on the movement, injected a pedantic quality into the body of original precepts through a series of liturgical exaggerations on the virtues of country life and the depravity of city life.

The original country-life movement died aborning. Congress, having grown recalcitrant toward an aggressive administration, turned a cold shoulder to the Country Life Commission, denied Roosevelt's request for $25,000 to print its report, and even went so far as to pass the Tawney Amendment which prohibited the appointment of similar commissions without congressional approval.[29] Yet, the impact of the country-life movement was enormous, albeit in a way unforseen and unintended by its originators. Beginning with Plunkett, Stowe, and Fiske, but extending well beyond them, the corpus of the original movement was subjected to a series of interpretations, each with its own amendments. The end result was a popularized version, bearing little resemblance to the original, that became the literary basis of the back-to-the-land movement. Its sudden appearance as a favorite theme in the popular magazines of the day hailed the beginning (perhaps renascence) of a national infatuation in America: dreaming of, talking of, planning for, and oftentimes actually undertaking a move from the city to the farm.

Yet, even before the back-to-the-land rhetoric began—in fact, at the very time the Country Life Commission was transmitting its report to President Roosevelt in January 1909—an important homestead bill was nearing final compromise in the halls of Congress. Its enactment a few weeks later reasserted the concept of homesteading within the public consciousness and no doubt quickened the heartbeat of hundreds of thousands of people who had been nurtured on the three-hundred-year-old American reckoning that there was free land to be had out West.

The Politics of the
Enlarged Homestead Act

The Enlarged Homestead Act of 1909 was a dry-farming homestead measure that provided for 320-acre grants of nonirrigable, nonmineral lands having no merchantable timber which were within the states of Colorado, Montana, Nevada, Oregon, Utah, Washington, Wyoming, and the territories of Arizona and New Mexico. (California, Idaho, Kansas, North Dakota, and South Dakota, initially included, were withdrawn upon request of their congressional representations.) Five years of continuous residence on the homestead was originally required, except in the case of some two million acres in Utah; and a graduated scale of cultivation was required. Commutation (buying title to the homestead after a specified period in order to hasten the ownership process, usually with the motive of making a quick sale) was prohibited. Authority for determining which lands were to be available for entry was placed with the Department of the Interior.[1]

The Enlarged Homestead Act underwent several important amendments during the first five years of its enactment. Chief among them were a reduction in the residency requirement from five years to three in 1912; an abandonment of the continuous residence requirement of twelve months per year, in favor of seven, in 1912; and the inclusion of Idaho and California within its provisions in 1910, North Dakota in 1912, and South Dakota in 1915.

As mentioned previously, this act has been criticized in a variety of ways by the leading historians of U.S. public land policy. The consensus among them is that it was based on a false assumption—that 320 acres of dry farmland was enough to provide an adequate living. As a result of the impracticality of the act, they argue, much mischief and heartbreak followed it. No challenge to these evaluations is offered here. The question to be explored, rather, is why Congress passed this enlarged homestead measure and why Theodore Roosevelt signed it into law. The view that a reckless West, unconcerned about conservation, outmaneuvered a reluctant East to gain enactment of the bill is either implicit or explicit in nearly all the standard works on public land policy. This view is the central object of the discussion that follows.

The Enlarged Homestead Act was based on many of the same assumptions reflected in the report of the Commission on Country Life. The report gave eloquent expression to the many virtues of farm life; the act provided both city and farm people with a means of either gaining ownership or enlarging their ownership, as the case may be, of farm land. Yet, only in the most indirect way can the Country Life Commission's report be considered influential in the passage of the Enlarged Homestead Act. The report was not transmitted to Congress until the very day that the act was passed, and there is no reason to believe that many senators or representatives had a sneak preview of it. Further, the report was given a chilly reception in Congress, and the House even refused Roosevelt's request for money to publish it. On the other hand, the report represented a reasonably thorough study and disclosure of conditions in rural America, and since most congressmen had rural constituents it may be assumed that they had some knowledge of these same conditions. It is likely that a number of congressmen were drawing the same conclusions as the members of the Country Life Commission about the actions that should be taken in response to these conditions.

The commission opened its report with a disclaimer of intent to influence the course of any legislation then before Congress—the enlarged homestead bill, for example—but several of its fundamental assumptions and the thrust of its message were unmistakably in the same direction as the homesteading measure. In speaking of the monopolistic control of streams as being one of the four leading handicaps faced by farmers, the commissioners wrote: "One of the very best elements of any population is the independent home-owning farmer, and the tendency of government, so far as may be practicable, should be toward securing the ownership of the land by the man who lives on it and tills it."[2] Moreover, the commission commended the Newlands Act of 1902, which provided for the financing of irrigation projects in the West through the sale of public lands, for its benefit to the West "not alone because it renders available for settlement large areas of previously worthless land, but still more because it insures to settlers the ownership of both the land and waters."[3] Finally, and not without promise for the future of a liberalized homesteading policy, the commissioners observed:

Even where there was once social organization, as in the New England town (or township), the competition of the newly settled West and the wonderful development of urban civilization have disintegrated it. The middle-aged farmer of the Central States sells the old homestead without much hesitation or regret and moves westward to find a greater acreage for his sons and daughters. The farmer of the Middle West sells the old home and moves to the Mountain States, to the Pacific Coast, to the South, to Mexico, or to Canada.[4]

Regardless of the congressional reaction to the recommendations of the Country Life Commission, there is no doubt where President Roosevelt stood. He had commissioned the study, had handpicked the members, and had given the completed report a vigorous endorsement. This in itself offers an important clue as to why he signed the enlarged homestead bill into law. Yet, there is more to it than that. The Enlarged Homestead Act had as its aim the opening of marginal lands to a highly specialized form of farming, a form that showed every promise of transforming those lands into a productive agricultural resource. As such, the act coincided exactly with Roosevelt's concept of conservation. "Conservation," he insisted, "is not keeping out of use, but is putting things to the best use without waste, and where possible, preserving their potential usefulness unimpaired."[5]

That Roosevelt sought a public land policy that would favor the individual owner, the actual homemaker, is incontrovertible. Time and again he voiced his conviction that the farmers were in the vanguard of conservation and that the movement of homesteaders westward was a healthy trend for the entire nation. Writing, for example, of his own cowboy days on the open range, he tempered his nostalgia with the following assertion:

It was right and necessary that this life should pass, for the safety of our country lies in its being made the country of the small home-maker. . . . The homesteaders, the permanent settlers, the men who took up each his own farm on which he lived and brought up his family, these represented from the National standpoint the most desirable of all possible users of, and dwellers on, the soil. Their advent meant the breaking up of the big ranches; and the change was a National gain, although to some of us an individual loss.[6]

In warming up for his Progressive campaign of 1912, Roosevelt commented that an essential feature of the country-life movement was conservation. He maintained that the natural fertility of the soil exceeded in importance all other aspects of resource management. But the impetus for this conservation would never come from urban areas, dominated as they were by big business. Rather, "it will come from the farmers who, alive to their duty in regard to the resources at their command, will see that they get their due share of those other resources which belong to the people at large, and to no privileged class."[7] In the latter stages of the campaign, Roosevelt carried this thought to an even more explicit expression. All the nation's natural reserves, he stated, should be handled and administered in the interest of "the actual settler, the actual home-maker." This man, the man who settles on his own farm and develops it, is working not just for himself but for posterity as well. "His permanent welfare," concluded Roosevelt, "is the prime factor for consideration in developing the policy of Conservation: for our aim is to preserve our natural resources for the public as a whole, for the average man and the average woman who make up the body of the American people."[8]

Roosevelt obviously took special pride in his contribution to the shaping and passage of the Newlands Act of 1902 which was the cornerstone of his reclamation program. With more than the usual amount of chest thumping, he pointed to the twenty-eight reclamation projects launched between 1902 and 1906—projects that involved the construction of huge dams, thousands of miles of canals, and tens of thousands of bridges and culverts. The end result was to bring precious water to some thirty thousand separate farms. Among the most significant of the many aspects of this achievement, according to Roosevelt, was its impact on the settlement patterns in the West:

> The population which the Reclamation [Newlands] Act has brought into the arid West, while comparatively small when compared with that in the more closely inhabited East, has been a most effective contribution to the National life, for it has gone far to transform the social aspect of the West, making for the stability of the institutions upon which the welfare of the whole country rests: it has substituted actual homemakers, who have settled on the land with their families, for huge, migratory bands of sheep herded by the hired shepherds of absentee owners.[9]

According to the Rooseveltian view, then, any measure that promoted individual ownership of western land was good for the West and good for the nation. An expanded homestead act for the semiarid West would obviously be right on target for him.

In addition to Progressive rhetoric, scientific advancements in dry farming had much to do with the politics of the Enlarged Homestead Act. The first decade of the twentieth century witnessed a resurgent optimism in dry-farming possibilities, an optimism that soared well beyond the initial enthusiasm of the 1880s. While much research had been done by various western state agricultural experiment stations since the mid-1890s, it was not until an independent researcher named Hardy Webster Campbell published his findings that dry farming gained wide public exposure. After fifteen years of research on farms in South Dakota, Nebraska, Colorado, and Kansas, Campbell published his first *Soil Culture Manual* in 1902. By the time of the publication of his second *Soil Culture Manual* in 1907, his name had become synonymous with dry-farming techniques.[10]

From a technical standpoint Campbell is easily faulted for failing to emphasize the need for developing new drought-resistant varieties of crops and for his continuous insistence that dry farms should be larger than 160 acres. More central to the point, however, is the way Campbell propagandized this renewed dry-farming movement through his reckless pronouncements on the certainty of its success. Typical is this view from 1902: "We do not believe we have reached the limit, but are hopeful that after careful experimenting we will be able to produce a yield that cannot be surpassed by any farmer in the more humid sections of Iowa or Illinois, and this is the semi-arid belt."[11] By 1907 his view of dry farming had become even more visionary. "There is no question in my mind but what the prairies of eastern Colorado, western Kansas, Nebraska and the Panhandle of Texas and a good portion of New Mexico—those regions I am more familiar with than the country farther north—can grow better average crops than they are growing in Illinois today, because we can secure the ideal condition, and control it, and they cannot do it in Illinois because they have too much rain."[12] In 1909 he expressed his conviction that the semiarid West was "destined to be the last and best grain garden of the world."

Campbell's optimistic assertions were widely quoted and paraphrased. They were carried not only in books and technical pamphlets but also in newspapers and organizational bulletins throughout the West. In 1906 they gained national circulation in the pages of *Century Magazine*.[13]

Hardy Campbell's heady influence on the dry-farming movement peaked in 1909. It declined sharply thereafter due primarily to opposition from E. C. Chilcott, director of the Office of Dry Land Agriculture in the U.S. Department of Agriculture. He labeled Campbell's pronouncements as "wild and extravagant" and publicly scolded him for the false impressions he had created. Chilcott was especially irritated that Campbell had gained a hearing in popular magazines, and he denounced "that certain class of popular writers" for their complicity in the matter. In public addresses as well as in Department of Agriculture publications, he argued that dry farming was a precarious business to be approached cautiously if at all.[14]

Chilcott succeeded in discrediting Campbell, but he did not succeed in discrediting Campbellism. In Montana, for example, Campbell's place as a promoter was quickly taken by Thomas Shaw, an agricultural consultant of the Great Northern and Northern Pacific railroads. Shaw continued to publicize dry-farming possibilities in the same vein as had Campbell. He shared the same basic conception, that dry-farm development was to be done on the level of the small, self-sustaining, and diversified farmer. Try as it might, the Department of Agriculture could not find an effective counterpoise to the dry-farm propagandists.

Moreover, the leading scientists of the dry-farm system agreed with Campbell on nearly all essential points. Certainly, John A. Widtsoe, director of the Utah Agricultural Experiment Station and a recognized pioneer in dry-farming research, saw eye to eye with Campbell, although he disputed the claim that Campbell was the "author" of the dry-farming system. Under Widtsoe's administration and scientific guidance the Utah Experiment Station became the center of initial dry-farm research in the Rocky Mountain West. A number of experts from surrounding states studied there, and much technical information emanated from it. In 1911 Widtsoe published a book entitled *Dry-Farming: A System of Agriculture for Countries Under a Low Rainfall* in Macmillan's *Rural Science Series* under the general editorial supervision of L. H. Bailey.[15]

Widtsoe's volume was a comprehensive guide to practical dry farming. Replete with photographs, charts, and drawings, it was written in a direct manner easily comprehendible by the layman. Select a farm of clay loam soil, he advised the would-be dry farmers, and make certain that the soil is uniformly structured to a depth of eight feet. He further urged location in an area with an annual average rainfall exceeding ten inches and that windy areas be avoided. "One man with four horses and plenty of machinery cannot handle more than 160 to 200 acres," he cautioned. "Farm fewer acres and farm them better."[16]

Widtsoe's appraisal of dry farming was not as sanguine as Campbell's, but it was still highly optimistic. He defended with considerable vigor his belief that dry farming would succeed even in drought years as long as proper procedures were practiced. "Always farm as if a year of drought were coming," was his dictum. He emphasized that dry farming was a highly specialized form of agriculture, one that required much work, skill, and intelligence. But he denied that it was a "precarious" business. He was openly critical of Chilcott's "conservative" attitude toward dry farming, charging that he had hindered the advancement of dry farming and had shackled the research resources of the U.S. Department of Agriculture.[17]

As an example of the success possible on a dry farm, Widtsoe pointed to the John R. Barnes farm in Kaysville, Utah. This ninety-acre tract, located in Davis County just north of Salt Lake City, had been dry-farmed since 1887. Barnes had kept careful records, year by year; and much of that data, through the year 1905, was charted by Widtsoe. The precipitation during those years varied from a low of 10.33 inches in 1890 to a high of 18.46 inches in 1889. The yield of wheat varied from a high of 28.9 bushels per acre in 1902 to a low of 12.5 bushels per acre in 1903, excluding 1888 which was the one year of failure. (Widtsoe ascribed this failure to improper soil preparation.) The chart reveals at a glance that yields in excess of twenty bushels per acre were the rule whenever the soil had been allowed to lie fallow the preceding year. According to Barnes's records, his net profit for the nineteen-year period was $5,257.14. Widtsoe concluded that this represented "a very fair profit" on the original $1,800 purchase price of the farm.[18]

Renewed enthusiasm for dry farming spawned its own special-interest group, which in turn publicized and promoted the dry-farming movement in numerous ways. This was the Transmissouri Dry Farming Congress. (The word "Transmissouri" was dropped from its name in 1909.) This group held its third annual conference, in Cheyenne, during the final week of February 1909, just a few days after passage of the Enlarged Homestead Act. Among the first items of business undertaken by the several hundred delegates were an endorsement of the Enlarged Homestead Act and the adoption of a resolution of appreciation to Congressman Frank W. Mondell of Wyoming for his efforts in securing its enactment.[19] The delegates seemed united in their conviction that the new homestead act would aid significantly in the development of semiarid lands, and Governor Shafroth of Colorado gave strong voice to that belief in his address to the conference.[20] The conference was oriented primarily in the technical direction, as seen by its concern and plans for gathering and disseminating dry-farming data on a worldwide basis. But by virtue of the very fact that several hundred people were meeting together within an organizational framework, the conference held political implications that were not ignored by important people in Washington, D.C. President Roosevelt sent a letter to the conference in which he offered his assurance that "any organization having for its purpose the development of the agricultural resources of the great semi-arid section of the United States should have the hearty support of all good citizens."[21] And just prior to the convening of the Dry Farming Congress, Gifford Pinchot wrote to it, asserting: "I am now and have been at all times greatly interested in the development of dry farming and confident that it would be of great importance to the west."[22] It was obviously with some justification that the *Salt Lake Tribune* could editorialize that "the Dry Farming congress has compelled the attention, not only of state governments, but of the national authorities at Washington."[23]

Senator Reed Smoot of Utah introduced the enlarged homestead bill into the upper house, and he defended and championed it through both sessions of the Sixtieth Congress. Initially, Senator Jacob Gallinger of New Hampshire led the opposition. His primary concern was that land granted today under the act may be brought within an irrigation project in the future, in which case a parcel of 320 acres would be much too generous. Smoot countered with the assurance that the bill was drafted to apply strictly to those lands which "no matter if a thousand years pass, they will never be irrigated."[24] This issue, defining the type of lands to be open for entry to ensure that they would be of the dry-farming variety and nothing else, was basic in the Senate debates. It was this consideration that prompted Senator William E. Borah of Idaho to press for insertion of the word "arid" in the section of the bill describing the lands available for entry. Smoot objected on the grounds that the word "nonirrigable" was explicit enough and that most western congressmen did not want the word "arid" used.

The Utah senator was not without support in his claim that the bill was drafted in terms explicit enough to avoid misunderstanding on the types of land available for entry. Senator Henry M. Teller of Colorado, for example, took the floor to inform his colleagues that there were thousands of acres of land that could not be irrigated even at a cost of a thousand dollars per acre, for water simply could not be procured unless carried in buckets.[25] And Senator Henry Cabot Lodge of Massachusetts warned that inserting the words "arid" and "semiarid" would introduce a most vexatious element of ambiguity and must therefore be avoided. The doughty eastern senator then expressed his belief that enlarging the homestead grants for nonirrigable lands, as proposed by the bill under discussion, would be "a good thing."[26]

At this point in the Senate debates it became clear where the real opposition to the bill lay: not in the East, Midwest, or South, but in the West itself. Specifically, it was Senators Borah and Weldon B. Heyburn of Idaho who debated the opposition viewpoint most vigorously. It is a matter of no small importance that they joined with Smoot and many other western senators in the desire to see the West attract new settlers. Yet unlike Smoot and other supporters of the bill, Heyburn and Borah felt that geographical conditions in their state were such that the Enlarged Homestead Act would actually work to restrict settlement there. According to Heyburn, Idaho was unique among the western states in that it had plenty of water and, therefore, an enormous potential for reclamation. He foresaw rapid development of irrigation projects under the Newlands Act, in which case new settlers could be expected to flow into Idaho in as large a number as available land would allow. "Three hundred and twenty acres of homestead is larger than we desire in Idaho," he announced. "We want more people than there would be represented by homesteads of that size."[27]

The passion of Heyburn's opposition to the bill explains why, during the course of four lengthy Senate debates, he was the only senator to mention conservation of natural resources in conjunction with the bill. One gets the impression that this was done only in desperation. Upon goading by Reed Smoot and Francis G. Newlands that Idaho's congressional delegation was not unanimous in the stand taken by its senior senator, Heyburn became indignant. He exclaimed in part:

> I heard some eloquent words here in regard to the preservation of the natural resources of the country, and I heard eloquent words about the forests that were to hold the waters and irrigate the lands. What becomes of that eloquence and the reasoning that was within it if you are going to give the lands to the land grabber? What is the use of conserving the waters of the country to irrigate the lands under those conditions?[28]

In the House debate on the enlarged homestead bill, the opposition was led by Congressman Paul Howland of Ohio. In both the minority report of the House Committee on Public Lands, which appeared over his signature, and in the debates, Howland hammered on the same theme:

> If the homesteader can not make a living on 160 acres of land, there
> is something wrong with the land or the homesteader. If the trouble is
> the land a greater quantity of that kind of land would not help the
> situation. If the trouble is with the homesteader the amount of land he
> enters cuts very little figure.[29]

On the other hand, Congressman Mondell, who championed the bill in
the lower chamber, quoted directly from a passage President Roosevelt
had sent to Congress on a previous occasion. "The land-law system which
was designed to meet the needs of the fertile and well-watered regions of
the Middle West has largely broken down when applied to the drier
regions of the Great Plains, the mountains, and much of the Pacific slope,
where a farm of 160 acres is altogether inadequate."[30] Howland objected
to this, pointing out that the president had been speaking of a grazing
proposition, not an agricultural homestead. It is unlikely, however, that
Mondell or any other supporter of the bill was embarrassed by Howland's
objection—for regardless of what the president had in mind on that particular occasion, it was their belief that the text of the quotation was factually
true. Congressman Marcus A. Smith of Arizona stated, for example:

> The West needs settlement. This [bill] will aid to some extent.
> Three hundred acres of the land described in this bill are worth less than
> 20 acres of irrigated land. There is no objection urged against it except
> by Eastern men, who never saw the public domain and who know noth-
> ing of western conditions.[31]

Smith's comment is worthy of particular note for two reasons. First, it
represented the clearest strain of an East-West lineup on the bill to be
voiced in the debates (a lineup not altogether substantiated by the House
vote on the bill; see table 1); and second, it reiterated the theme around
which Smoot in the Senate and Mondell in the House had built their case:
the Enlarged Homestead Act would certainly aid in attracting more settlers to the West. Mondell was particularly explicit in that regard:

> This is a bill more in the interests of the constituents of every Mem-
> ber on this floor than in the interests of my constituents, except that
> some of their constituents may, under this law, become my constituents.
> It is an enlarged homestead for those we hope will come to help us
> conquer the desert.[32]

Nor was the Wyoming congressman open to charges of attempting to
feather his own nest at the expense of his midwestern or eastern neighbors,
for as the Commission on Country Life had pointed out, farmers through-

TABLE ONE

Vote Distribution on the Enlarged Homestead Act in the U.S. House of Representatives

	Ayes (140)	Nays (74)	Answered Present (12)	Not Voting (150)
Alabama	6			3
Arkansas	4	1		2
California	4			4
Colorado	3			
Connecticut	2			3
Delaware	1			
Florida				3
Georgia	4	1	1	5
Idaho	2			
Illinois	10	5	2	7
Indiana	5	1		6
Iowa	5	2		4
Kansas	2	5		2
Kentucky	3	2	1	5
Louisiana	2			4
Massachusetts	3	5		6
Michigan	2		1	9
Minnesota	4	1		4
Mississippi	4	1		3
Missouri	8	5		3
Montana	1			
Nebraska	5			
Nevada	1			
New Hampshire	2			
New Jersey	1	3	2	6
New York	11	5	1	19
North Carolina	2	3		4
North Dakota				2
Ohio	1	11		9
Oklahoma	4			1
Oregon	2			

Continued on next page

Table 1—*Continued*

	Ayes (140)	Nays (74)	Answered Present (12)	Not Voting (150)
Pennsylvania	6	5	3	17
Rhode Island	1	1		
South Carolina	1	4		2
South Dakota	2			
Tennessee	4	6		
Texas	8	3		5
Utah	1			
Vermont	1			1
Virginia	6			4
Washington	3			
West Virginia	1	1		3
Wisconsin	2	2		
Wyoming	1			

Source: 11 May 1908, *Congressional Record*, 60th Cong., 1st sess., 6098.

out the country were not hesitating to leave their present homes in search of greater acreage elsewhere. Though Mondell probably had not yet seen that report, he obviously was aware of the trend. He pointed out to his House colleagues that homesteaders had been moving west continuously but that in four cases out of five they had been forced to abandon their 160-acre claims within three years. The dislocated homesteader then returned "to his folks or his wife's folks in Missouri and Iowa and Illinois," Mondell concluded. "He has not done us any good and we have not done him any good."[33]

Howland seems not to have been particularly opposed to Mondell's conclusions, but he remained firmly opposed to his premise that the problem could be solved by enlarging the homestead. His assumptions were remarkably similar to those expressed by Heyburn in the Senate. In one of Howland's final observations on the bill, he remarked:

> The more homes that can be established on the public domain the better for the country at large and the particular Commonwealth in which the homestead is located. This bill, however, by doubling the

acreage of the homestead entry, provides for only one-half as many home-steaders as would be taken care of under the present law.[34]

Howland then predicted that the country would soon experience a land famine, asserted that the policy of government "should be to conserve our resources," and urged that the enlarged homestead bill be defeated. This was the only instance in the House debate in which voice was given to the concept of conservation. There, as in the Senate, it was simply not a significant part of the opposition argument.

Only in the House was a roll call taken on the Enlarged Homestead Act, the "sectional" nature of which is reflected in table 1. With the exception of California's delegation, the representatives of the western states were solidly in favor of the measure, whereas representatives of the East, South, and Midwest were split widely in all directions. Obviously, the bill could have never passed had it not been for substantial support lent by nonwestern congressmen. Any evidence tending to support the claim that the Enlarged Homestead Act was a sectional issue is scanty indeed.

Editorial comment of the *Salt Lake Tribune* on the act was lukewarm at best. It voiced the belief that the promoters of the measure were not necessarily subject to the charge of intending to enlarge the opportunities for land fraud and further postulated that the measure would be watched with great interest throughout the West, that there would be some fraudulent acquisitions, certainly, and that there would be contests between claimants and forest reserve officials. "In a general way we should say that the working of the law ought to be for good, but whether it will pan out that way or not remains to be seen."[35]

One might safely assume that Senator Heyburn was looking directly at Senator Smoot when, near the conclusion of the final debate, he fumed: "The idea of standing up here and boasting their zeal to preserve the public land against the spoiler; the idea of standing up here and boasting their zeal to preserve the natural resources of the country, and then giving their support to a land grabbing measure of this kind, is beyond my comprehension."[36] For the truth is that Reed Smoot, who sponsored the Enlarged Homestead Act and defended it so vigorously, also considered himself to be in the vanguard of the conservation movement. As a historical proposition this is not without considerable justification. Two days prior to the passage of the Enlarged Homestead Act, Smoot had secured a promise of an appropriation of $25,000 for the National Conservation

Commission. The following day he was invited to a conservation conference at the White House attended by delegates from Canada and Mexico,
where he delivered one of the welcoming speeches. The next day—the day
the enlarged homestead bill was passed—he was invited to dinner at the
Pinchots, a dinner held in honor of the Canadian and Mexican delegates on
conservation, where he gave still another speech. And it was Smoot who
took the lead in pressing for increased forest appropriations that year. He
spent two days preparing his Senate speech in defense of that cause, which
he delivered just one week after the passage of the Enlarged Homestead
Act, and which took nearly three hours, with interruptions, to complete.
The appropriation not only carried, but Smoot was also successful in
defeating an amendment offered by Senator Teller which would have
released certain forest reserves from federal control. "Teller told me he
would punish me for it," the Utah senator wrote in his diary, "and [he]
was very wrathy."[37]

It appears evident, then, that the members of the Sixtieth Congress did
not view the Enlarged Homestead Act as contravening the principles of
conservation. Only once in the Senate debate and only once in the House
debate was the concept of conservation introduced in argument against the
act, and these instances were obvious reflections of frustration and desperation. Further, on the respective issues of the enlarged homestead and
increased appropriations for the Forest Service, the pattern of voting
among seven leading western senators does not sustain the hypothesis that
the two were opposites. Such substantiation could have come only if the
senators had aligned themselves in one of two ways—in favor of the
Enlarged Homestead Act and opposed to increased forestry appropriations, or opposed to the Enlarged Homestead Act and in favor of increased
forestry appropriations. Only Henry M. Teller of Colorado and Thomas
H. Carter of Montana aligned according to the first alternative, and only
Frank P. Flint of California aligned according to the second. Smoot,
Heyburn, Borah, and Warren do not fit the model.[38] Moreover, it will be
recalled, Smoot championed *both* issues.

Similarly, the supposition that the Enlarged Homestead Act was an
East-West sectional issue does not stand up under scrutiny. Voice was not
even given to that thought in the Senate debate. Only once in the House
debate was expression given to a sectional lineup, but such was not sus-
tained by the distribution of votes there. Further, in the Senate proceedings the most adamant opposition to the measure did not come from the

East but rather from the West, and both Idaho and California specifically requested to be excluded from its provisions.

The Enlarged Homestead Act did not emerge from a vacuum. In large measure it proceeded from significant advancements in scientific farming. The research and writing of such figures as Hardy Webster Campbell and John A. Widtsoe had gone far in convincing interested parties that dry-farming techniques could be applied successfully to millions of acres of semiarid land then lying dormant. No one could have been attracted to this proposition more than Theodore Roosevelt, whose notion of conservation centered around scientific use and management of natural resources. Given his devotion to the homesteader, it is easy to understand why he signed the Enlarged Homestead Act into law.

The Back-to-the-Land Movement

During the last week of October 1913, an obscure federal official reached into a huge lottery bin and withdrew an application. The name on the application was read and recorded. Again the official reached, drew, and read. The process was repeated until 531 applications had been withdrawn for that many sections of free land from the North Platte Forest Reserve and a military reservation in northwestern Nebraska. Seventy-five thousand hopefuls had applied. Never had a land lottery attracted so many applicants, a source of amazement to many in view of the quality of land involved. Nearly two-thirds of the land was deemed useless for any purpose except grazing. True, a handful of the parcels were valued at several thousand dollars apiece, but it was still estimated by one source that the cumulative expense incurred by the applicants in filing vastly exceeded the total value of the land.[1] Certainly, by the advent of the New Freedom, the back-to-the-land passion was rampant in America.

The back-to-the-land movement was a bastard child of the country-life movement. Unlike its parent it had no perceptible intellectual base, no patron saint. Its bent was primarily emotional, and it affected a much larger number of people. It became a sort of national infatuation. The seventy-five thousand who hoped to receive a free section of Nebraska land were just a few of the participants in a much larger drama.

Demographically, the back-to-the-land movement operated on two distinct levels. Many of the participants were interested only in a rural residence in the country, a home with a few acres of ground where they could grow fresh vegetables and perhaps a little grain and hay for the support of a few chickens and three or four cows. These were gentlemen farmers. They tended to locate within easy commuting distance of the city in order to maintain their regular employment. Commercial farming was not their aim.

The other level of the back-to-the-land movement involved those who aspired to be commercial farmers, men who also sought inexpensive land, but in much larger units than the gentlemen farmers. Many of these—perhaps most—never made it back to the land, for one reason or another. Yet, for a period of several years, aspiring to become one's own proprietor on one's own farm was a preoccupation with a large segment of the American public.

It is impossible to date exactly the beginning and end of the phenomenon, but the back-to-the-land movement ebbed and flowed for at least two decades. The movement began during Theodore Roosevelt's second term as president and remained strong throughout the 1920s. The year 1932 witnessed a greater return to the farm than any of the previous twelve years, and on that basis the movement may be viewed as extending to the advent of the New Deal. Yet, it could be argued that the forces impelling people farmward during the Great Depression were unique. Certainly, many of the people who moved to the farms during the depression did so out of desperation—as an alternative to prolonged unemployment and despair or even hunger.

Assigning a numerical dimension to the back-to-the-land movement is also difficult. Figure 1 presents a useful graphic representation of movement after 1920, but unfortunately no such data are available for the period 1910 to 1920; the Bureau of Agricultural Economics was not created until 1922. Even the fourteenth decennial census reports are silent on that matter.

Even the graphs for the period after 1920 do not define the entire breadth and depth of the back-to-the-land movement. They reveal the substantial number of persons who actually left urban areas for rural areas, but they say nothing about how many aspirants failed to make the move. Presumably, the latter greatly outnumbered those who actually relocated. The aspirants who did not move were as important as those who did, in terms of exerting pressure on president and Congress for an enlarged homestead policy. These data are also mute on the subject of motivation. They reveal nothing about why people sought a return to the soil, or how they came to think they could slip into a business such as farming, where experience and liquid capital are important ingredients of success.

The purpose of this chapter is to examine the back-to-the-land literature in search of answers to these questions. The popular magazines are the medium since it was through them that the movement gained its widest exposure and its most vigorous expression. The survey of articles that follows is not intended to be exhaustive but rather a representative sampling of the thought expressed on the subject. For the most part they have

FIGURE ONE

Movement to and from Farms, 1920–38

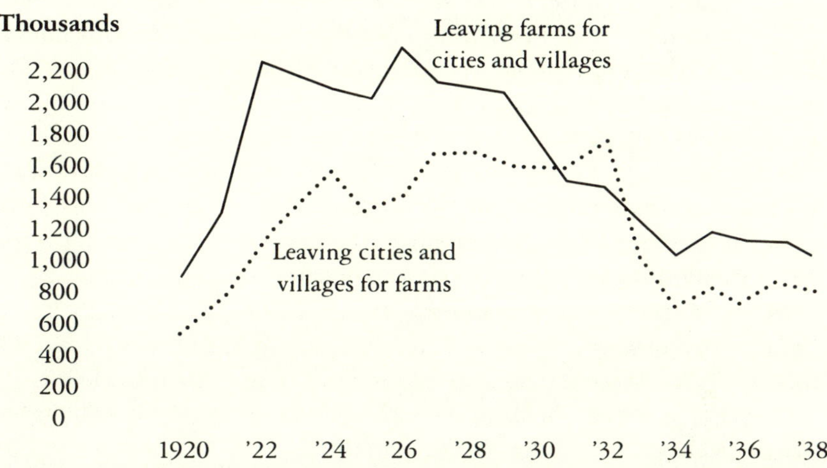

Source: U.S. Department of Agriculture, *Statement on Farm Population Trends*, prepared for the Bureau of Agricultural Economics by Conrad Taeuber (Washington, D.C.: Government Printing Office, 1940), 6.

been selected from the period between 1909 and 1916, since these were the years of the passage of the Enlarged Homestead Act and the Stock Raising Homestead Act, respectively. Thematically, the literature includes not only the gentleman farmer and the commercial farmer but a third type as well, one that may be viewed as an extreme version of either of the other two: the woman homesteader.

" 'Back to the country' is a topic more than ever before discussed and dreamed about by city people," began a *Collier's* article in 1910.[2] The rising expenses and accelerating pace of city life are prompting large numbers of city dwellers to seek a simpler and saner environment, it continued, and this has already "turned a tide of migration toward the village and the farm." Consequently, announced the editors, they would begin a regular serial on the movement. Projected for future publication were such articles as "The Amateur Farmer's Chances of Success," "The Cost of Equipping a Country Home," "Building Up an Old Farm," "Making the Garden Pay," "Managing Five Acres," "The Live Stock of the

Small Place," and "The Children and the Farm." The article by Ralph D. Paine, "Finding a Country Home," was the logical beginning.

According to Paine, there were several fundamental considerations one should keep in mind when shopping for a country home. Most basic was that of practicality rather than sentimentality. A rock field and a moss-covered roof might look enchanting, but they meant trouble. A farmhouse built in a hollow was likely to be unbearably hot in the summer. One situated in the lee of a hillside was certain to be damp and unhealthy. No house should ever be bought, regardless of its location, until its frame had been inspected and found to be sturdy. Finally, a plentiful supply of water was the most important consideration of all.

With these considerations in mind, the prospective buyer of a country estate should look for one equipped with a barn, coops, and storage sheds. A barn of sufficient size to house hay, livestock, and vehicles might cost as high as four thousand dollars to build. A coop might cost as much as three hundred. The aspiring farmer should seek an estate with a wood on it, for he could then cut and haul his own firewood for $2.50 per cord (approximately one-sixth the cost of buying it in the city).

In shopping for a country estate, Paine continued, the city man must be careful to select one with a large garden plot near the house. A gently sloping hillside plot was best, but a well-drained field would do. A garden would represent a savings of three hundred dollars per year on groceries. The coops must be large enough to house fifty hens and three hundred pullets. This much poultry would save a family a hundred dollars a year. A pasture for two cows should be included. In addition to keeping the family supplied with dairy products, two cows would produce an additional seventy-five dollars' worth of dairy goods above the cost of feed. Room must also be made for the lowly pig. He might be bought and raised for ten dollars; when butchered he was worth four times that sum. A sizeable orchard was also desirable; with careful maintenance it could produce five hundred dollars' income every year.

With no difficulty, insisted Paine, it could be proved that a thousand dollars in the country is worth twice that much in the city because of the many opportunities for trimming expenses. Few who established their little farms would ever return to the city. But life in the country was more than peace and quiet and a reduction in living expenses; it was independence. "It was the 'embattled farmers' who drove back the redcoats from the redoubt on Bunker Hill," he reminded the readers.[3]

Throughout the year, and beyond, *Collier's* continued to feature regular articles on new gentlemen farmers. But by the end of a year the tone of the articles had changed. They had slipped beyond the practical to the promotional, beyond the restrained to the sensational. In "Taking the Plunge," featured in the *Collier's* issue of March 11, 1911, author Ernest Russell drew a parallel between the first man to jump into the swimming hole (while the others gingerly wet their toes and dawdled on shore) and the man who had already left the city for a country residence. Russell, having taken that plunge, urged his diffident brethren to join him. The water is fine, was his message.

Perhaps the greatest deterrent to taking the plunge, according to Russell, was the expense involved. But that argument, he insisted, had no validity. After all, an ideal ten-acre farm, one with a brook, a pond, and a nearby wood, could be purchased for two thousand dollars. Further, the natural advantages of such a farm—health, restful surroundings, and the charms of nature—could never be had in the city at any price. To the dawdler who feared a sudden amputation of city conveniences, Russell offered his personal assurance that the country of today had its stores, markets, libraries, theatres, churches, and icemen. For the man who feared the prospect of losing an hour a day on the commuter train, the author insisted that commuting would soon become a welcome experience; it gave the person a chance to be alone with his thoughts, a time to plan.

Another consideration to be kept in mind included the desirability of year-round living. The full benefit of life in the country could not be felt by the sometime dweller there. In this regard, it was a wise man who located near a town that offered both electric- and steam-car service to the city. But in the matter of school for the children, no special considerations were required. Nearly all country schools had responded well to the recent impetus for improved education, and, indeed, had done so with fewer complications than most city schools with their crowded conditions and "mixed nationalities." Nearly every country town had a school equipped to educate a child to age fifteen. Besides, insisted Russell,

> It is not from books alone that your children receive an education—and a valuable one—in the real country. The country is, after all, but a great natural open-air gymnasium; in its freedom, its constant occupation of mind and body in healthful activities, it is the one place in the world for children to make their real start in life. They will experience there, as nowhere else, an unhindered development of thought and action; become intimate with external nature, the wild life about them, and the vicissitudes of the weather and the seasons; enter early into the life itself, and with ax and spade and hoe assist in wholesome labor.[4]

For the timid city dweller who had suddenly found the fortitude to actually make the move, Russell offered several tips. First he should locate on a farm beyond the "automobile-haunted thoroughfares" for his family's comfort and safety. Second, he should locate in the high places, assuming water was available, in order to enjoy the pleasures of space and view. Next, he should be careful not to overly exert himself during the initial stages of farming. The primary object of owning a country estate was to enjoy its wholesome surroundings. Financial rewards would materialize not only because of "lower rentals, of lower commodity prices, and the use of self-raised food-stuffs, but the equally important economies that follow a condition of life removed from the artificial standards of the city."[5] One would become less extravagant about clothing; toys, trolley trips, and similar amusements would become unimportant. The physician would be needed less often.

Many of the themes expressed in the *Collier's* articles were also reflected in the various personal reminiscences about country estates. One of the more engaging examples of this type is "Wayback," by Susannah J. Keeney, published in the *Independent*.[6] The family involved in this article had a two-year-old child afflicted with whooping cough. The doctor's prescription that she must live outdoors seemed hardly feasible in their New England manufacturing town, beclouded as it was with black smoke from a dozen industrial chimneys. So, for a beginning, the family went on picnics at regular intervals, but the logistics involved (stove, ice, kettles, hammocks, raincoats, and the rest) soon turned these outings into drudgery. Luckily, on one such picnic the family discovered an abandoned and dilapidated shack at the edge of a lake. The mother immediately saw it as the answer to the family's needs. The father sought out the owner and made him a satisfactory purchase offer. The parents then rolled up their sleeves and went to work. The roof was raised, the stairs rebuilt, small rooms were made into large ones, and additional windows were framed in. New wallpaper was hung, floors and fireplaces were scrubbed, and new cupboards were installed. Finally, a broad veranda, screened with wire netting, was built around three sides. The family moved in.

The new homestead was a joy from the beginning. Lying in their beds at night the family was lulled by the lapping waves on the shore, by the solo of the whippoorwill, the serenade of the hylas and katydids, and the bass obbligato of the frogs. During the day the children knew absolute freedom of space ("perhaps the greatest advantage" of life there), grew wise in the secrets of nature, maintained a variety of pets in their spacious domain, and "grew strong and straight and fearless." What is more, all this had been gained at minimal expense. The cost of buying, repairing, and maintaining the country retreat was small in comparison to periodic trips to health resorts. There was also the saving in clothing. At "Wayback" the mother could shop in the attic "instead of laying in a stack of fashionable garments." And with the extension of the trolley line to the far end of the lake, the father no longer had the expense of driving the family car to work every day.

Articles relating to the hobby-farmer or country-gentleman aspect of the back-to-the-land movement spanned the spectrum of popular periodicals. Yet, the contemporary student who desires an in-depth immersion into that genre need go no further than one magazine. Its entire format was devoted to that subject alone. Beautifully done on 10-by-14-inch glossy paper and loaded with high-quality photographs, the magazine was appropriately titled *Country Life in America: A Magazine for the Home-maker in the Country*. It was published by Doubleday, Page & Company on a monthly basis from the beginning of the century until 1910, then on a semimonthly basis until 1912, then again monthly until 1942. Significantly, Walter Hines Page, a member of Theodore Roosevelt's Commission on Country Life, was co-owner of the company; L. H. Bailey, chairman of that commission, was one of the magazine's earliest editors.

In the March 1, 1911, issue of *Country Life in America,* the editors referred to a letter recently received from Mr. F. D. Coburn, secretary of the Kansas Board of Agriculture, in which the writer insisted that there was no back-to-the-land movement. The editors admitted to being startled over this information since they "had been hearing a lot" about such a movement. So they investigated, concluding:

> Oh, there's a back-to-the-land movement, all right. In fact, it is amounting almost to an epidemic in some places, and the time has already come for a word of restraint. Mr. Coburn ridicules the city man's farm dream, and often it is ridiculous. But the city man has this dream, and we may as well recognize it and do what we can for the poor chap.[7]

Therefore, continued the editors, a special edition of their magazine— the next issue—would be devoted to that end. It promised to be an optimistic and inspiring issue, one reflecting enthusiasm for the movement and encouragement to the city man hoping to make the move. Still, it was to be thoroughly conservative, painting no rainbows; it would simply point out the best chances for achieving success on the farm.

Of special significance is the issue of March 15, 1911, which featured such articles as "The Landward Movement" (by none other than L. H. Bailey), "Could I Succeed on a Farm?," "The Philosophy of the Soil," "A Five-Acre Model Farm," and "Cutting Loose From the City." Not entirely in keeping with the pledge of the editors but consistent with the established format of the magazine, each of these articles was oriented toward the aspiring gentleman farmer—the city man who hoped to buy a few acres in the country, create a country estate, plant a vegetable garden and a small orchard, and keep a dozen head of livestock.

Bailey, in his "The Landward Movement," remained true to the basic tenets of the country-life movement. One need not read further than the first three paragraphs to recall the essence of his familiar message:

> Two movements are now much in evidence—the country-life movement, and the back-to-the-land movement. They are not only distinct, but in many ways antagonistic. The country-life movement is the effort to make the real farming regions as progressive and as effective in a social and economic way as are the cities and towns. The movement is thoroughly sound, because any effort to increase the efficiency to an existing civilization is sound.
>
> The back-to-the-land movement of the towns is the effort to place city people and towns-people in farms. It is in part an effort to relieve city congestion, in part the expression of the desire of city people to escape, in part an effort of real estate people to sell land. For the most part, the movement is unsound as a corrective of city ills.[8]

Denouncing the "fashion of periodical literature just now to exploit and pictorialize the farming business," Bailey reiterated his belief that people desiring to flee the city should content themselves with hobby farms—country estates from which they could commute to their established place of employment in the city. If they did not have the financial means for that, or found the idea unsatisfactory for any other reason, they should consider the possibility of moving to the country in the capacity of a technician, assuming of course that they were professionally qualified. Rural America was in desperate need of more ministers, doctors, teachers, lawyers, recreational advisers, marketing experts, home economists, and many other professionals. If that were not a viable or attractive alternative to the disenchanted city dweller, if he were still determined to become his own proprietor on his own commercial farm, then his only logical course of action was to spend as much time and money as necessary, before moving, to gain a complete education in agriculture. This must include some practical farm experience as well as college courses.

The message of A. P. Hitchcock in "Could I Succeed on a Farm?" was very close to Bailey's. To the businessman who asked that question, Hitchcock would answer with a similar question: Could I, as a farmer, succeed in your business? Farming had become a highly technical and complex vocation, was his point, and one would court disaster by jumping into it without the requisite knowledge and skills. Hitchcock's advice was that a city dweller should not leave his present job in favor of commercial farming. True, he himself had done just that twenty years ago, but he would not wish on anyone the frustrations and discouragement he had experienced during his early years on the farm. Only after he had begun to concentrate on truck farming had his income risen above the subsistence level. The urbanite who was determined to return to the soil and could afford a small place should find suitable challenge and satisfaction on a hobby farm.

"The Philosophy of the Soil," by David Grayson, was a paean to the natural beauty of farm life and the magnificence of farm work, obviously oriented toward the gentleman farmer. ("Somewhere on every farm, along with the other implements, there should be a row of good books.") Grayson's basic thesis, familiar to the serious student of this genre of literature,[9] is that the city is not man's natural habitat and life there will cause him to atrophy. The great tragedy is that most city dwellers either do not recognize their atrophy or else lack the courage to do something about it:

> Men and women there are—the pity of it—who, eating plentifully, have never themselves taken a mouthful from the earth. They have never known a moment's real life of their own. . . . They take *nothing* at first hand. They gather the odor of odors, not the odor itself; they do not hear, they overhear. A poor, sad, second-rate existence! Bring out your social remedies! They will fail, they will fail, every one, until each man has his feet somewhere upon the soil![10]

The city worships standardization, insisted Grayson, while the country encourages diversification. City life demands manual training, but country life develops initiative, industry, discipline, and a variety of skills. Only in the country can a lad experience natural and complete development.

For some time, "Cutting Loose from the City" was a regular serial in *Country Life in America*. One such piece, by William B. Hunter, was subtitled "How Cooperation Helped Four City Business Men and Their Families to Establish Ideal Country Homes in Georgia, and to Develop a Peach Orchard that Will Eventually Yield Them All a Permanent and Generous Income."[11] With the assurance that all these serials were true accounts, the editors introduced them as personal histories of people having "the courage to break away from life in the city and start anew in the country."

The gentleman-farmer aspect of the back-to-the-land literature followed a basic pattern. Generally, these articles began with a look at the decision of the man to leave his residence in the city for one in the country. It was never an easy decision; the individual was certain to be plagued with doubts and anxieties. The unmistakable message was that the timid never made it. Most articles then devoted a good deal of space to describing the renovation of the old farmstead. Father, mother, and children put on their old clothes, grabbed hammers, nails, rakes, shovels, brooms, and paintbrushes, and went to work. They developed blisters on their hands and they knew the discomfort of sore muscles, but they reveled in the spirit and delight of being creative and productive, of watching the dilapidated house and outbuildings turn into their own genuine country estate. Emphasis was also placed on the freedom enjoyed by the children in their spacious realm and the new vistas open to them for education under nature's tutelage. They and their parents invariably became healthier and stronger in this salubrious environment. Much stress was also placed on the economics of living in the country. There was not only the great savings involved in producing one's own vegetables, fruit, and meat and dairy products, but there was also the added economy of lower housing expenses, fewer doctor bills, and less expensive clothing.

These articles nearly always contained elaborate descriptions of the joys experienced by the family in coaxing life from the soil. It was at once challenging, educational, and exciting. It prompted the proprietor to rise at 4:00 A.M. in order to work in his garden a few hours before having to leave for his job in the city, and it was the greatest source of his pleasure upon returning in the evening. He knew for the first time the exhilaration of being a producer. Finally, all these articles reflected contempt for the city. Cities were noisy, rapacious, crowded, impersonal, and expensive— everything the country was not. They restricted privacy, befouled the air, stifled creativity, and forced conformity to the standards of the masses.

Many of the themes expressed in reference to gentlemen farmers were also prevalent in the various articles on new commercial farmers—only expressed more forcefully. Especially conspicuous were the themes of physical therapy, monetary reward, freedom, adventure, and the opportunity for creativity and initiative. Typical in terms of both style and content is "Back to the Farm on Fifty Dollars: An Autobiography," which appeared in a 1913 issue of *Sunset*.[12] Unlikely as it may seem in view of the title and the first-person construction of the article, the author's identity is not disclosed. Indeed, its very authenticity is suspect.

"Back to the Farm on Fifty Dollars" was recounted by a man whose business in St. Louis had collapsed. Extricating himself with nothing more than a knapsack of clothing, fifty dollars in cash, a case of tuberculosis, and a determination to own his own farm, he left Missouri for the Sacramento Valley. During his first week in California he met only discouragement. His two contacts there, including a brother, refused to assist him; his money gave out and he began to experience hunger. Then his luck changed. Near the small town of Gridley he found the opportunity he had hoped for: leasing fifteen acres of farm land on a half-crop basis and purchasing an additional five acres at $150 per acre with the first payment deferred for five years. The owner of these twenty acres agreed to loan his tenant money for lumber, tools, and equipment if he, in return, would level the fifteen acres suitable for irrigation and plant part of it in alfalfa, part of it in orchard. The agreement was struck and recorded in a written contract. "This gave me a chance, a fighting chance, and that was all I asked," the anonymous author crowed.[13]

The narrator went on to describe how he built a two-room house, a stable, two chicken coops, and a storage shed. This, and the digging of a well, he did with his own hands. He then borrowed money to buy a team of horses, a variety of implements, and household furnishings. In a section of his reminiscences subtitled "The Beauty of Being in Debt," he listed his various expenses, including the purchase price of the five acres, as two thousand dollars. He was not worried about the resources required to liquidate the debt. His land was producing nine tons of alfalfa per acre, and alfalfa would bring ten dollars per ton. His garden produced vegetables in abundance, especially tomatoes and melons which "pay big profits." Then there were the chickens. In California, chickens lay eggs year round, and eggs "command a good price." Further, he had no difficulty finding contract employment with his team of horses, and the wages were good—four dollars for a nine-hour day.

A year after leaving St. Louis the author had cause to rejoice. He had his own farm and was making it pay. He had known the joy of meeting a challenge and the pride of achievement. "My garden is the finest in the country, and . . . I am especially proud of my orchard." He had experienced the moral rejuvenation of being successful and the physical rejuvenation of hard work in the open air. It would be a calloused reader who did not feel a twinge of envy upon reading the concluding remarks:

> I have succeeded in making it back to the farm with fifty dollars. The uncertain period is past. The foundation is now laid. I control the situation. From now on my little ranch will produce enough to keep me in comfort, furnish funds for further development and also pay for itself. Best of all, I am today a strong healthy man doing each day as much work on my ranch as any of my neighbors does on his, and if I did not fear that some of them might see this story I would say that I think I am doing a little more. It would be a brave doctor, indeed, who would risk saying that I have tuberculosis now.[14]

Several of these themes, particularly those of creativity, adventure, and pride in achievement, were reflected in a 1910 *World's Work* article.[15] Typical of much of the back-to-the-land literature, this article will strike most modern readers as implausible. "The Farm Boy Who Went Back," is Johnny Wortman's story. Johnny grew up on the farm and he hated it. He hated the long working day, the nature of the work, and the barren social outlets of rural life. He hated the poverty and the cruel tricks that nature played on farmers. Immediately after his mother's death, Johnny left the farm. For the next several years he bounced from place to place and job to job in search of challenge and reward. Roustabout, dishwasher, secretary, hod carrier—Johnny was each of these and more. To New York, Salt Lake City, Portland, even Brazil, the young man went. He knew hunger, cold, physical abuse, and despair. The little money he had managed to accumulate vanished overnight in an ill-advised speculative scheme. With that, his health failed. Tuberculosis, said the doctors.

Johnny, out of alternatives, returned to the farm. But with him he took a certain conviction garnered from his recent experiences: brains and toil could produce incredible results. Suddenly intoxicated with this idea, he approached farming with a determination to master all its secrets. He started with geese. Relentlessly and voraciously he studied geese. He studied them in pamphlets and he studied them in actuality. Soon he knew the various species by nomenclature, by disposition, by fertility and growth rates. From that point it was a short step to the development of a new type of feed ("a judicious mixture of grass, grain, roots, cabbage, beef scrap and pure water") which cut the length of the fattening period by 25 percent. From geese Johnny turned to corn. The results were again extraordinary. Patiently, scientifically, tenderly, he experimented with new ways to produce corn. Through detasseling, hand pollination, careful grading, and storage under controlled conditions of temperature and humidity, he was able to produce a superior quality of seed corn which had neighboring farmers "coming a-running" to see for themselves. From corn his attention turned to installing tile pipe to draw excess water from clay soils. Again the results were little short of revolutionary. Everything young Johnny touched seemed to turn to gold. Obviously, there was much more than a dollars-and-cents consideration to Johnny's commitment. For what it may be worth, however, he was making as much money from his forty acres as others were from six times that many.

In reference to commercial farmers, the matter of monetary reward was treated in a variety of ways. A few articles suggested that with a bit of pluck and luck there was virtually no limit to the money the commercial farmer could make. Others suggested that farmers should reconcile themselves to a life of relatively low income but that they could expect to reap a rich harvest of intangible rewards. Still others, perhaps a majority, struck a middle view by arguing that while farming was not the sure road to wealth it was a business from which one could expect to make a comfortable living.

Typical of the latter view is a 1910 *Collier's* article, "Unreckoned Values in Country Living."[16] According to this article the aspiring farmer need not be particularly concerned about the low income level commonly associated with the agrarian sector of American society. Per capita income reports were misleading when applied to farmers because they revealed nothing about the "unreckoned values" of life on a farm. In other words, living expenses were much lower in rural areas. Through a highly questionable series of arithmetical calculations the author (unnamed) arrived at the conclusion that "compared with the dweller in town, the farmer lives almost rent free." Where a city man may have to pay as high as six hundred dollars for a flat, a farmer could live in a twelve-room house at an annual expense of a hundred dollars. Perhaps even more significant was the savings in groceries available to the farmer. With little effort he could produce a wide variety of garden and dairy products. Again, through the application of suspect mathematics, the author concluded that a farm family of five could produce all its required vegetables, fruit, eggs, dairy products, and meat for a total of $335.92 per year.

That was not all. Urban society seemed to demand that a family be dressed fashionably and expensively. Never was clothing to show signs of wear or age if one were solicitous of societal approval. On the other hand, country people could be sensible about such matters, could purchase clothing with an eye for durability rather than fashion, and could, without embarrassment, wear this clothing until its only logical inheritor was the ubiquitous scarecrow. Still another unreckoned value inherent in farm life was that of nominal medical expenses. Admittedly, this was not easy to calculate, but it was certain that urbanites were spending millions of dollars annually on vacations to the open country for the purpose of regaining their flagging health. It would be easy, continued the article, to find many cases similar to the professional man whose family medical bills ran as high as two hundred dollars per year in the city but dropped to two dollars during their first year on the farm. Half of that expense went for the treatment of a cut finger, the other half for a prescription to treat a trifling cold.

Collier's also had an answer for the city dweller who desired to remove to the farm but hesitated for want of farm experience. From a 1913 article one would get the impression that every farm district was aswarm with agricultural experts whose sole purpose was to advise individual farmers on the latest scientific and efficiency techniques.[17] Many of them were retained by the U.S. Department of Agriculture, many others by state agricultural departments, some by state colleges, and some by counties. They were an amazing group of men—abiding, devoted, energetic, and very expert. Such an advisor was Professor John S. Collier of the University of Illinois.

> In the course of a day's work he will address two or three gatherings in villages or at country schoolhouses and visit half a dozen or more farms. One hour he will be talking about the advantages of deep plowing with one farmer, and the next he will be inspecting the poultry yard of another. He may stop at a barnyard and show a milkmaid the best method of draining a cow's udder, or climb over an orchard fence and tell a fruit grower how to keep his trees healthy. Frequently he is called upon to size up a blooded horse or give his opinion on a newly imported bull.[18]

The back-to-the-land urge was even compelling enough to lure clergymen from their calling. Such was the case with the Reverend William Justin Harsha, whose account was published in the *Outlook*.[19] At age fifty,

Harsha had entered a critical phase of his emotional development. He had become increasingly distraught by a nagging suspicion that as a clergyman he had grown "stale." After lengthy soul-searching he concluded that "since a minister is, like all men, a son of mother earth," a return to the soil was the logical and most likely source of rejuvenation. With that he and his tubercular son each filed homestead entries in a sage-covered bowl near Middle Park, Colorado.

Harsha's narrative of his early homesteading experience is typical of most such accounts. It is a story of initial discouragement (the gophers destroyed the first year's grain harvest), of greenhorn mistakes (using green logs instead of dry ones in the construction of the cabins), and of the usual frustration in learning to work with livestock. It does offer an intriguing glimpse into homesteader-cowboy relations, however. At first the cowboys viewed the Harshas as curiosities, as strange people attempting the impossible because they lacked the sense to know better. But when it became plain that the homesteaders were determined to stay, the cowmen launched a short but spiteful program of harassment which included shooting the Harshas' pets, stealing their calves, and stampeding their colts.

But the Harshas persevered and came to enjoy a modest prosperity. Within a few years they had 640 acres under cultivation and lived in an eight-room house. They developed mechanical skills, in which they took inordinate pride, grew tan and healthy, experienced the joy of a sound night's sleep, and discovered the pleasure of breakfast. The results were naturally positive, both physically and spiritually. "I am ten years younger than I was a dozen years ago," asserted the elder Harsha. But that was the least of it. Having repaired "to the desert for a time of meditation," he, too, had learned to know and value life. He had, in short, found the emotional rejuvenation he needed. He had no regrets about having abandoned the cloth. "I am content and thankful that I took Uncle Sam at his word and hit the trail to the brush," he concluded, "for my inner manhood has come to its best."[20]

Another clergyman to abandon the cloth in favor of the soil was Arthur Markley Judy. His reminiscences, published in a 1915 issue of *Atlantic Monthly*,[21] adumbrate the central theme of Harsha's account and in fact meld together many of the views on farm life. They also reflect a thorough familiarity with the writings of L. H. Bailey.

For twenty-five years following his ordination, Judy had served as minister of a large midwestern city church. During that time he had enjoyed a wide range of professional and social experiences bearing on his cultural development. He had also worked diligently at the physical side of his development, conscientiously devoting time to golfing, rowing, walking, and playing tennis. The same may be said of his intellectual life. As a minister he had taught classes, promoted lectures of various types, and had developed a fine personal library. He felt confident that he had enjoyed most of "the best that the associations of a city can yield."

Soon after leaving the city for the farm, however, Reverend Judy came to discover that his total development had barely begun in the city. Seven years of "hard knocks" on the farm clearly constituted the better part of his education when compared with his seven years in the academic community. His farm experience had resulted in "the development of manhood . . . as amazing as it was unexpected."

Perhaps the most pleasant discovery to Judy, the one in which he seemed to take the greatest pride, was that the rigors of farm work had given him hardiness. Within a short time after his removal to the farm he viewed his former physical fitness program as "laughable." But of a much higher qualitative order than hardiness, according to Judy, was the moral courage which farming developed in a man. The farmer is a man who dares. He dares to control the face of a planet. He dares to defy the caprices of weather. He dares to war against insects, bacteria, and churlish soil. In short, he dares to lose, and because of this he can know the magnificence of victory (success) in a way unimaginable to the clerk, the mechanic, or the professional.

Compassion, continued the narrator, is another virtue bred of farm experience. The farmer's livelihood is intimately linked to his draft animals and other livestock. He worries his mind and exerts his body in their behalf. From this experience the farmer is likely to develop an even greater compassion for his fellow human beings, and human fellowship is the rock to which true democracy is anchored. Similarly, farming teaches reverence for nature and expands one's capacity for the appreciation of beauty. Whether it is in the gracefulness of a colt or the color of a wheat field before harvest, the message is the same and the sensation is never lost to the man who deals with nature for a living. According to Judy:

> Nine tenths of all the men in the city with whom I have spoken
> about the farm have expressed an eager desire to be farmers. It is, I
> think, really not that they wish to be farmers—to do the business and

produce the fruits of the farm, for of that they know not whereof they speak; but it is that they hear the call of their elemental being, they feel the hunger of manhood for its first home—the vast open, the gleam of the untainted sky, the odors of the sod, the turmoil and conflict of the body with things, the thrilling revelations which the rough tutelage of nature forces on the expanding soul. Lacking these, they are dimly conscious that the best in life is lacking.[22]

Not only in terms of style but in content as well, Judy's article represents a level of sophistication rare among the back-to-the-land writers. He recognized, for example, that there were many farmers in the nation who were not "earning wages." Further, he insisted that the many virtues he had associated with farming would not develop automatically. Indeed, "one finds on the farm a large proportion of men and women of exceptionally poor character." By neither ignoring these facts nor attempting to gloss over them, the author stepped beyond the mainstream.

But to the Iowa farmer who only made $164 profit last year or to the Illinois farmer who could not raise the money to buy phosphate fertilizer, the Reverend Judy could promise that if they were progressive people they would reap a harvest of intangibles vastly exceeding anything they could find in the city, that the glory of life lay not in spending but in producing. To the city dweller contemplating a move to the farm he could say, do not flee failure there in the assurance of finding success on the farm, and, above all, do not leave the city for the farm without having done your homework. But if possessed with character, genuine motivation, and the appropriate technical education, anyone could become a farmer and know the exhilaration of complete personal development.

Particularly revealing of the length to which the back-to-the-land movement extended was the large number of articles reflecting the theme of "lady homesteader makes good." Here, as in all other aspects of the movement, there were greater and lesser degrees of sophistication. Among the more extreme examples of this genre is an article by Mabel Lewis Stuart that appeared in a 1913 issue of the *Independent* under the title "The Lady Honyocker: How Girls Take Up Claims and Make Their Own Homes on the Prairie."[23] Asserting that "the west needs forming as much as the city needs reforming," the article stresses the opportunities for humanitarian service awaiting the lady homesteader in the vast stretches of Montana, Wyoming, and the western Dakotas. Instances are portrayed of indomitable feminists scampering "over cactus and sage brush and thru deep draws" to participate in temperance meetings, teach school, nurse the sick, direct the church choir, or even to speak from the pulpit.

Of special significance is the fact that the article makes no mention of the physical aspects of farming. How one was to make a living is not clear, but apparently the task is neither arduous nor time-consuming.

> Varying interests claim the time and attention of the homestead girl. The musician practices three hours a day on her piano, does her homework, drills the choir, tends her poultry and garden and has some time left for her favorite pastime of target shooting. Household duties are more or less exacting on the claim, and girls who come out with the idea that life will be one long holiday are surprised to find how busy they are. If one is to live and if the frequent visitors (one girl counted fifteen in one week) are to be properly fed, bread must be made, the cookie jar kept filled, and other important details attended to. Before the cooking can be done there is also wood to be chopped from the huge pile before the door—it is possible for a girl to become a very good woodchopper.[24]

Also significant about this article is its suggestion that feminine homesteading was the fashionable thing to do. Claiming that the courage and independence of the lady homesteader had already won for her the applause of modern chivalry, the article even includes a ballad written by Arthur Chapman in her honor.

Of the same strain is a *Collier's* article by Mary Isabel Brush, "Women on the Prairies: Pioneers Who Win Independence and Freedom in Their One-Room Homes." As the subtitle suggests, this article portrays homesteading as an avenue of escape from the societal strictures faced by the American woman.

> As for going back to that life of dependence—she drew herself to every inch of her four foot nine—she should not think of it. Her father tried to dictate to her whom she should marry, and what was more important, whom she should not. And she considered that was something to be decided in one's own heart. Besides, it was always that same sort of dependence; that giving way to her father, her brothers, to the deacons in the church, to the directors of the school! Ugh! She loathed it! She wished to be free—free! And she loved farming. She was never going to sell her claim. She liked to get out in the fields and work![25]

The suggestion is strong that women homesteaders must be prepared to face physical labor, but no mention is made of the toll that farm work exacts from the feminine physique. On the contrary, such activity is pictured as being of cosmetic value. The "grass widow" who returns home for a visit is certain to amaze her old friends with her renascent beauty— "so sunburned, and the little lines from around her mouth and eyes are all gone!" After she has ridden her dedicated little mustang to Cheyenne for the Frontier Day celebration, she "swings freely out of the saddle, fresh and eager for the activities of the day. Her hands are as brown as the leather wristlets she wears, and the flame color in her face does not pale beside the scarlet of her silk handkerchief, drawn loosely around her neck."[26]

Typical of this genre, "Woman on the Prairies" conveys the message that homesteading is the popular thing for women to do. Widows, divorcees, the unbetrothed, stenographers, and society ladies—virtually everyone, it would appear—were moving west to take up a claim.

More plausible is an account offered in the *Overland Monthly* of January 1916. In this article a woman schoolteacher recounted her experience as a dry-farm homesteader near Ft. Benton, Montana. "I felt that I had every qualification for farming that a man has except the brute strength," reasoned this feminist homesteader, "and I argued that that was the cheapest commodity to hire."[27] Even at that she would never have dared undertake the venture had she not enjoyed the assurance from "Uncle Sam" that she could continue in her salaried teaching position while proving up the claim. For additional moral support she entered into a working partnership with her brother (a successful homesteader) and another woman teacher.

Their first house was constructed of two railroad boxcars, purchased at a cost of $110 each. Fortunately, they located adjacent to a railroad and, by baking lemon pies for the trainmen, were able to keep themselves supplied with ice and coal during the first summer.

Returning to school in the fall, the teachers hired a man to break forty acres. The next spring they had it planted in flax which yielded seven bushels per acre for a gross profit of a hundred dollars. Using their teaching salaries for capital they also renovated their dwelling and dug a well—for a combined total of $250. That spring they planted a garden that produced an abundance of fresh vegetables, and by the end of summer they had arranged to break another forty acres.

The teacher-homesteader offered some intriguing dollars-and-cents data in her reminiscences. By the end of five years she had poured nearly three thousand dollars into the venture. In turn the homestead had produced approximately seven hundred dollars as a gross profit, and of that amount four hundred dollars had been disbursed for hired help. Besides having spent five hundred dollars per year of her teaching salary on the farm, she had also found it necessary to borrow another five hundred. Ostensibly, these figures would have discouraged the most determined land seeker. But there was the other side of the ledger which the author also shared. By the time her entry was carried to patent the farm was valued at thirty dollars per acre. Even the more sluggish arithmeticians among her readers could have determined that for a 320-acre homestead this represented a total value of $9,600, or a 300 percent appreciation in a five-year period. Further, the entire farm was fenced, and over half of it was planted in wheat, oats, and alfalfa with a promise of heavy yields. In addition, the homesteader owned several fine horses, two cows, several dozen chickens, a coop, cellar, wagon, carriage, harnesses, and other implements.

The article closes with a word of guardedly optimistic advice:

> The farms that Uncle Sam has to give away need very careful manage-
> ment in order to make them into paying propositions. They are merely
> opportunities, not certainties. I advise most teachers to stick to their
> jobs. Those who have a longing for the simple life can buy a few weeks
> of that kind, which consists of picking flowers and eating vegetables
> fresh from the garden, but for those who have the real farm hunger,
> there is a way 'back to the land.' As for myself, I know of no other way
> by which, in five years' time, I could have acquired such riotous health,
> secured such valuable property, experienced so much joy in living, and
> infused so much hope and buoyancy into life, and no other way to
> provide such cheering prospects for my old age.[28]

Using a different approach to tell a similar story is a serial of letters from a woman homesteader appearing in six issues of *Atlantic Monthly* from October 1913 to April 1914. According to the editor's introduction, the letters were genuine, written to a friend without thought of publication. They were written by a widow, Elinore Rupert, who accepted employment as a housekeeper for a Scottish cattleman in Wyoming. (She later married him and took the name Stewart.) Her intent was to use the job as a means of subsistence for herself and her two-year-old daughter while establishing her own homestead. The published letters—several dozen in all—tell a wonderfully entertaining story full of romance, humor, and adventure.[29]

In contrast to the theme of joy and success reflected in Mrs. Stewart's letters is that of discouragement and anxiety expressed by Anna W. Case in her letters to the family, printed in *Overland Monthly* in 1918.[30] This series lies somewhat beyond the "woman homesteader" theme—Mrs. Case was in the company of her husband—and extends beyond the chronological range of the Progressive Era. It is mentioned here, however, for what it discloses about the intensity of the back-to-the-land commitment despite the physical rigors and emotional trauma involved in the search for a homestead.

The Cases' search for a homestead took place not in the western United States but in Canada. They traveled by train for the most part but had to resort to horseback and stage to reach prospective homestead sites. They and their three children were constantly tired and often sick. Further, each site they visited seemed less promising than the previous one. From Pouce Coupé, British Columbia, Mrs. Case wrote that the water was fatally alkaline, a noxious weed jeopardized livestock, the southern region of the province was subject to drought, the northern region produced early and late killing frosts, and the central region was notorious for devastating hailstorms.

After several weeks of fruitless searching, the Cases returned to Edmonton, Alberta, deeply discouraged. Of this dilemma, apparently shared by hundreds of others, she wrote her sister-in-law:

> We are almost ten years too late to get a desirable homestead, and it is too bad so many people keep coming here for this purpose, only to be disappointed. Every day they are coming—from Washington, Arizona, Kansas, Ontario, Norway, etc. The Immigration Hall where we were staying became crowded for rooms, and as our seven-day allowance was passed, we felt like an immigrant, for at the Immigration Hall we all found ourselves in the same boat, whether American or Norwegian.[31]

Within a month, however, the Cases had decided not to spend the winter in Edmonton but to move to Vancouver Island. There they hoped to buy a ten- or twenty-acre tract and turn to the production of loganberries. With much of the western United States and Canada having gone "dry," Mrs. Case foresaw an increased demand for fruit juices. Already, she observed, loganberry juice was wholesaling for fifty cents a quart.

By the end of the second serial, then, the Cases had abandoned the hope of homesteading and were heading further west to make their fortune on a loganberry farm. Mrs. Case closed her letter with the conviction that no one who had shared her experiences would ever try to locate a homestead. Interestingly enough, however, she also reaffirmed her determination to remain away from the eastern United States forever. "If we had $10,000," she informed her sister, "I do not think we would go any further east than southern California."

Somewhere in nearly every basic textbook on American history, the student is advised that with the Gilded Age, rural Americans started moving to the cities in significant numbers, that this trend accelerated to the point that by 1920 the population of the United States was predominantly urban, and that the swing from rural to urban America has continued to the present day. What these texts seldom mention is that this demographic shift did not proceed on a one-way street. There was a heavy flow of population in both directions—from the country to the city and from the city to the country—during the first three decades of the twentieth century. On balance, more people flowed into the cities than out of them, but beginning in the first decade of the century, and rolling into the second under a full head of steam, was a collective passion—indeed, an emotional contagion—among many urban Americans: to gain ownership of their own tract of farmland. This was the back-to-the-land movement, and a very sizeable movement it was.

The back-to-the-land movement gave birth to a new genre of literature, one that had the effect of further reinforcing the demography of the movement. As expressed in the popular magazines of the day, this literature has been surveyed for what it discloses about the movement, for the insights it may offer regarding the motivations, aspirations, and assumptions impelling the movement forward. Whether the principal was a gentleman farmer searching for a few acres just outside the city, a commercial farmer who hoped to make a living from the soil, or an unattached woman seeking independence on her own homestead, the literature reflects certain basic and recurring themes. Generally, these themes are expressed with little sophistication and little variety. They are expressed straightforwardly, even bluntly. Like the movement itself, there is nothing subtle about its literature.

One of the most persistent themes of the back-to-the-land literature is that country life is salubrious. It makes sick people healthy, weak people strong, old people young, and young people mature. Life in the country cures tuberculosis, whooping cough, anemia, and a variety of other physical maladies. It revitalizes one's appetite but keeps him lean. It promotes longer and sounder sleep at night which increases a person's productivity during his waking hours. It sharpens a person's physical senses. Odors, flavors, sounds, and sights are suddenly startling in their intensity. Life becomes a first-hand experience. Similarly, working with nature opens entirely new vistas for aesthetic appreciation and lends an extra dimension to the wonders of creation. It teaches one humility and compassion.

Life on the soil also opens new channels for creativity. One becomes his own architect, carpenter, and master painter. He can know for the first time the incomparable joy of producing life from the soil with his own hands. He can, if he wishes, become a scientist and experiment in the production of new varieties of crops. He can take pride and satisfaction in genuine achievement. He is certain to expand his problem-solving ability and to learn patience and discipline.

To live in the country is to live free. Particularly is this so with the unattached woman. Unburdened by outmoded societal norms and unreasonable family strictures, she is free to express herself as her own individual. But in the country, freedom is also the luxury of the man, his wife, and their children. It is freedom from the counterfeit standards of the city, freedom to romp, freedom to be oneself.

A plot of land is also money. It is money in the production of crops and livestock. It is money in the form of reduced living expenses. Savings in groceries, housing, clothing, recreation, and doctor bills makes one country dollar worth two city dollars. A person need not be greatly concerned about going into debt to start a farm. Sufficient money will soon be produced from the soil to repay the loan. There are experts out there to show the newcomer how it can be done.

Little wonder, given these promises, that large numbers of urbanites sold their city residences and moved to the country. Little wonder that president and Congress came under increasing pressure to accommodate them. An elected official could hardly afford to ignore such a broad social undercurrent. Not surprisingly, during the administration of Taft and Wilson there was much talk in Washington about a new homestead law.

The Politics of the
Stock Raising Homestead Act

The Stock Raising Homestead Act of 1916 provided for homesteads of 640 acres of nonirrigable lands that contained no merchantable timber and were valuable primarily for grazing and the production of forage crops. Mineral and coal rights were reserved by the government, as were watering places and related access ways. Cultivation was not expected, but as a precaution against speculation the act required improvements of $1.25 per acre to be placed on the entry before a patent could be obtained. At least half of such improvements had to be completed within three years of entry. Commutation was prohibited. Authority for designating which lands were to be open for entry was placed within the Department of the Interior, with the act specifying that designation to be limited to that class of land of which 640 acres were "reasonably required" to support a family.[1] Clearly the act was restricted in its geographical applicability to western portions of the United States, particularly the Rocky Mountain and Great Basin regions.

The bill providing for grazing homesteads was drafted, publicized, and introduced by Congressman Harvey B. Fergusson of New Mexico. A reading of the congressional hearings on the bill confirms Professor Gates's observation that Fergusson's commitment to the bill was more passionate than rational. Fergusson, for example, can be criticized for his intransigent opposition to any scheme of land classification, for his failure to grasp the necessity of water to service the homesteads he was campaigning for, and for the naiveté of his optimism regarding the productive capabilities of the semiarid public lands.[2] Given the popularity of the back-to-the-land movement in America at that time, however, Fergusson's limited vision during the hearing is not surprising. Few people, congressmen or otherwise, seemed willing to look at land ownership introspectively during that period. Repeatedly, Fergusson advised the committee that his constituency was howling for this piece of legislation. As a sample of the correspondence he had received from the voters back home, he introduced into the hearings over a hundred letters and some seventy petitions urging immediate passage of the bill.[3] The number of signatures on the petitions varied from seven "citizens of Curry County" to 1,600 "citizens of Union County." Signatures numbering in the sixties and seventies were common.

The various letters and petitions received by Fergusson from his fellow New Mexicans show little similarity to the popular rhetoric on land ownership discussed in the previous chapter. These messages made no reference to the magic healing powers of life on the soil, no testimonials to the opportunity for creativity on the farm, no paeans to the cult of Apollo and Artemis. They were much more visceral than that. The vast majority of these communiques were written by (or from the standpoint of) New Mexican farmers and stockmen, many of whom were original homesteaders. It is not entirely clear whether Fergusson deliberately chose to emphasize that viewpoint, but the consensus within those letters and petitions is clear. Typical of most is the following, written by R. G. Bryant of Portales:

> I was very glad to read that you had introduced a bill enlarging the homestead entry to 640 acres; it is what this country needs to bring it to the front; our people can not run enough stock on a half section to do much good, but with a full section you will see this side of the State fill up with farmers pretty fast.[4]

The petitions reflected one or more of four basic claims: that tracts of 160 or 320 acres were not of sufficient size to provide for a family but that tracts of 640 acres would be; that until tracts of 640 acres were easily available, prospective settlers would have to shun New Mexico and present settlers would be forced to either leave the state or find another means of livelihood; that if the public domain were placed under a leasing arrangement rather than a system of enlarged homesteading, the large cattle interests would soon become dominant over the "little man"; and that beef production would increase and the entire stock industry would stabilize with grazing homesteads of 640 acres. Predictably, most of the substantive oral testimony presented to the committee—not only by Fergusson but by the other members and witnesses who were friendly to the bill—included one or more of these themes.

It had become apparent by the spring of 1914 that an important change in public land policy was near. The hearings before the House Committee on Public Lands included not just one bill, but two. The first was H.R. 10539, introduced and championed by Congressman William Kent of

California. Its aim was to provide a broad system of leasing of the public grazing lands, under which title to the lands involved would remain with the federal government. The other was the Fergusson bill, H.R. 9582, which proposed to grant actual ownership of grazing lands, in 640-acre parcels (mile-square sections), to homesteaders. Both bills were predicated on the same assumption—that the existing system of free grazing was obsolete. Uncontrolled grazing, it was agreed, had inflicted heavy damage on the public domain to the point of jeopardizing not only the natural resources involved but the western cattle and sheep industry as well. The proponents of both bills agreed that something had to be done to rectify the situation. Their differences centered on the means, not the end.

Hearings on these two bills were held consecutively, with the Kent bill being heard first. The rhetoric showed little variation from one hearing to the other. Throughout, Kent, a cattleman himself, contended that leasing was the surest means of restoring the carrying capacity of the public grazing lands. For support he pointed to the success achieved within the national forests under a system of grazing leases. Fergusson, on the other hand, argued that the surest means of restoring the carrying capacity of these lands was to place them under private ownership. For vindication he pointed to the Kinkaid Act. Within the huge gap separating these basic assumptions, the debate proceeded with each side pandering to its friendly witnesses, interrupting and otherwise harassing opposing witnesses, and exchanging barbs.

Obviously, the matter of conservation was inextricably linked to the basic issue. After all, it was because of the depleted condition of the public grazing lands that these bills had been drafted in the first place. But the most that can be said of the issue of conservation as debated in these hearings is that both sides saw their bill as being the best suited to restoring and conserving the natural resources involved. This fact was so plain throughout the hearings that the word "conservation" was seldom used. One of the few times the word was mentioned was in an exchange of ideas between Congressmen Frank W. Mondell of Wyoming and John E. Raker of California, both of whom favored an enlarged homestead measure over leasing. It illustrated the folly of semantic debate and probably explains in large part why the word "conservation" was generally avoided.

> *Mr. Raker.* From your statement which you made a while ago, in regard to the great quantity of forage going to waste in the Eastern States, and

your statement as to the use of the ranges in the West, would you say
there has been as much conservation in the East, so far as forage is
concerned, as in the West?
Mr. Mondell. There has been very much more conservation in the East
than in the West, if conservation means conserving a thing to go to
waste.
Mr. Raker. Mr. Mondell, you have had enough experience to know that
I do not mean that.
Mr. Mondell. I would like to have your definition of conservation. If a
complete utilization of a product in a useful way is conservation, no
place on earth has had better conservation of its natural growth than the
range country in the West.
Mr. Raker. I agree with you on that; and have not all these stock and
cattle which have come from these ranges assisted in building up the
country and making more prosperous the farmers and people living in
that community?
Mr. Mondell. Oh, yes; if it had not been for the stock business, in a
stock State like ours, we would not have had much of a State.[5]

To reiterate, the proponents of the Kent and Fergusson bills differed
not on the end but only on the means. Both were committed to conservation. The question was whether federal administration or private ownership would best promote it.

The House Committee on Public Lands consisted of twenty-one members. They were well distributed geographically, representing sixteen
states and one territory. A number of the representatives did not participate actively in the hearings, however. Indeed, Congressman Kent stood
nearly alone in defense of his bill. Level of activity aside, the committee
was predisposed to the Fergusson bill from the outset. The back-to-the-
land urge, then rampant in America, had made the idea of homesteading a
highly popular political subject.

Naturally, the members of the Public Lands Committee were aware
of, and often made reference to, the rapidly accelerating demand for
land ownership in the nation. For example, in his testimony before the
committee, Assistant Secretary of the Interior A. A. Jones spoke of the
number of U.S. citizens who were leaving the country each year to find
farms in Canada. Here at home, he observed, applications for homesteads were numbering nearly sixty thousand per year under existing
law. Since the best land had already been taken, the rate of failure
among the new homesteaders was high. But, Jones related, even poor

land and a strong prospect of failure were not enough to deter these aspiring homesteaders. In this regard, Congressman Denver S. Church of California referred to data recently presented to the committee showing that 138,000 applications for homesteads had been submitted the previous year (1913). Jones thought that figure was incorrect, but he again acknowledged that the demand for homesteads had greatly outrun the supply of suitable land, with unfortunate results for the more recent homesteaders.[6]

Proponents of the Fergusson bill knew they had a friendly witness in Secretary Jones and they made the most of it. Mr. Raker, for example, asked Jones: If the present demand for land continued could it be assumed that very little public land would remain in another twenty years? Jones answered:

> That would undoubtedly follow if they were to continue. I think the greatest trouble now is in preventing the people from taking up these lands under laws which are not applicable and under which they can not support families. I think we are inviting disaster in many, many cases, and these lands will go to patent under existing law, a great many of them; I certainly feel that simply indicates the great demand that there is for homes and that we ought to provide some means for giving them good homes.[7]

Raker then asked if the solution lay in increasing the size of the homesteads such that the applicant might have a better chance for success. "That is my opinion," was Jones's reply.

The explanation of why the committee was disposed to Fergusson's bill goes somewhat beyond the fact that Americans were clamoring for easier access to land ownership. There was also the matter of the traditional American distrust of federal efficiency as compared to private initiative. Congressman Kent could not convince his doubting colleagues that federal machinery would be more efficacious than private enterprise in restoring and preserving the carrying capacity of grazing lands. His claim that federal management of grazing lands within the national forests had been strikingly successful was compromised by Fergusson's charge that only the large cattle interests had benefited from that program. The fact that the American National Livestock Association endorsed the Kent bill probably hurt his cause more than it helped. On the other hand, the proponents of the Fergusson bill presented much favorable testimony in support of their claim that one who owns land is likely to dedicate his entire life and all his resources, both mental and physical, toward developing that land. For incentive, he had his very livelihood. This conviction repeatedly surfaced during the proceedings, but it was A. A. Jones who expressed it best:

> The natural tendency in the West, and especially in New Mexico, where we have a great many private land grants to deal with, has been to divide those large holdings, and it is noticeable there—I think generally throughout the State—that the man with the smaller area is getting more out of it in proportion than the man with the large area. The man with a small area will manage in many ways to get more out of his property. He will develop the water in different localities, so that the cattle will not have to go so far for it. He will build trenches out of little draws so that the water will spread over a considerable area and increase the grazing capacity, or perhaps enable him to grow some forage crops upon it. He will take better care of his animals, he will breed them up better, he will get a larger percentage of increase than a man handling live stock on a larger scale.[8]

The first witness called in support of the Fergusson bill was Congressman Moses P. Kinkaid of Nebraska. It was he who had introduced the homesteading measure, passed in 1904, that provided for 640-acre homesteads in western Nebraska. Early in his testimony he was asked by Fergusson, "Has your act been a success in settling up your State in this semiarid region?" Kinkaid replied, "Taking the judgment of the people who live in the territory, it has proven to be a remarkable success."[9] Similarly, Congressman Mondell, who by 1914 had gravitated to the position that homesteads of 1,280 acres were required in the semiarid West, testified that the 320-acre Dry Farm Homestead Act had worked "exceedingly well" in his state of Wyoming.[10]

Kinkaid and Mondell could hardly be considered unbiased witnesses. Obviously, they could not have been expected to acknowledge anything but success in the operation of their respective homestead laws. But this type of testimony is common in congressional hearings; unbiased witnesses are a rarity. The aim of the proponents of the Fergusson bill was largely to build a case for private enterprise.

The stock raising homestead bill was debated thoroughly both in committee and on the floor. The procedural and substantive provisions of the bill as well as the intent and workability were explained, questioned, defended, and rebutted. But much of the House debate also reflected a striking resemblance to the popular rhetoric on the back-to-the-land movement. Many of the themes expressed in the popular periodicals were employed by the supporters of the bill. That life in the country offered moral and physical rejuvenation, that it fostered creativity and afforded freedom of action, that it sharpened one's aesthetic appreciation—all were reiterated in congressional debate.

Romanticizing the agrarian way reached its extreme example in remarks offered by Congressman Church of California.

> This bill is calculated to take people out into the foothills where can be produced almost all that is consumed; out where a person can sleep at night, where children are happy and on horseback ride to school, where father works the farm and mother trades the eggs for groceries at the store, where brother learns to hunt, fish, and swim, and sister sews and sings and entertains her beau. [11]

Church continued in this mawkish vein at length. In recalling childhood memories of life on his father's homestead in California, he expressed gratitude that the ranch had been located "away from the strife and din of the city, where the flowers nodded and the meadow lark sang, where the quail whistled, the ground squirrel scolded, and the sad dove moaned." It was from that idyllic setting, he assured his listeners, that he had received his first notions of the pure and the sublime, and it was from the surrounding mountains, upon which shone the moon and stars, that he had received his first impression of God.

Variations of this theme were offered by Congressman James V. McClintic of Oklahoma, who expressed his conviction that tracts opened under the act would be settled and developed by "thousands of sturdy, energetic, patriotic, and loyal citizens,"[12] and by Congressman Charles H. Burke of South Dakota, who quoted from a prediction by a prominent Wyoming figure, I. S. Bartlett, that the act would "settle up the vast area of waste lands in the nation with a hardy, intelligent, and progressive American citizenship."[13]

Such adjectives as sturdy, loyal, cheerful, honest, and patriotic were used often by the bill's supporters in describing the type of man who had homesteaded in the past and who could be expected to homestead in the future. Regarding the latter adjective, at one point in the debates Congressman Scott Ferris implored Congressman James R. Mann to "search into the innermost recesses of his heart" in order to find some patriotism with which to support the bill. [14]

On the other hand, the debilitating effect of city living also found expression. The following quotation from Congressman Church could have easily appeared in any of the back-to-the-land articles discussed in the previous chapter:

> I am in favor of any bill that takes people away from the cities into the great outdoors to build for themselves homes. In the country home nearer than in any other place we find content. Our cities are filled with perplexities and unrest; the grind of machinery, the noise of the factory, and the shriek of the locomotive keeps the nerves of the city man strung to the key of G. [15]

Church further asserted that the act, if passed, would bring happiness to hundreds of those "saddened hearts" in the cities, who, feeling they had failed in life, would suddenly have a chance to begin anew. His conclusion was that the act would "bring color to faded cheeks, merriment to many a cheerless tenement child, and place a new star in the dark life of many hopeless men."[16]

A variant of this theme was offered by Congressman Charles F. Reavis of Nebraska, who suggested that in every community across the nation there were wage earners constantly haunted by the realization that creeping age must surely end their employment and that these men were hopeful of accumulating a piece of property on which to sustain themselves when that evil day should come.[17] Somewhat less explicit was Congressman McClintic's remark that "if there is any class that your Government should help it is those who have not been fortunate enough to provide for themselves a little domicile which they could call 'home.' "[18] And Congressman Fergusson, upon reporting the bill from committee, asserted that the proposed homestead measure would afford "an outlet to the congested civic and labor centers of our population without driving homeseekers to take advantage of the liberal land laws of Canada."[19]

Those congressmen who supported the proposed homestead bill also placed much emphasis on the economic opportunities that would be opened under it. They stressed those in or little above poverty as being the most likely beneficiaries of the act, and here they departed somewhat from the mainstream of the back-to-the-land genre of literature. Yet, reminiscent of that literature, the congressional supporters of the bill did not mention the handsome amount of capital required to launch a farm irrespective of the cost of the land.

The assumption of many of the bill's proponents seemed to be that whatever favored the poor individual would hinder the rich corporations, and much was made of this claim in the debates. Here, too, the congressional rhetoric departed from the popular literature. By the same token, however, it drew very near the spirit of Woodrow Wilson's New Freedom. Congressman McClintic, for example, noted that the nation's history was full of examples of intimidation and violence having been heaped on those who undertook to fence off a portion of public lands for the purpose of establishing a home. This he offered as a reminder of the age-old story that unless restrained by a higher order "the mighty will crush the weak."[20] He also insisted that there were thousands of people waiting, watching, and hoping for a chance to better their present condition. His assumption was that the proposed act would present just such a chance. Congressman Benigno C. Hernandez of New Mexico (successor to Fergusson on the latter's death in 1915) foresaw the act as coming to the rescue of the "humble and lowly" in a much more effective manner than antitrust legislation ever could.[21] And Congressman Kinkaid assured his colleagues that he favored an enlarged homestead act over leasing because the former was based on the rule of "the greatest good to the greatest number."[22]

In this regard, Congressman Burke quoted from a report issued by Charles D. Wolcott, former director of the U.S. Geological Survey, charging that where homesteads of insufficient size were allowed, eventual abandonment by the settler could be expected; and the general case in the past had been for such lands to drift into the control of corporations.[23] Congressman Eben W. Martin of South Dakota pointed out that the average farm size in several western states was similar to that contemplated under the act. "We have never had a land monopoly in this country," he claimed, "and we never will have so long as Congress remains wise enough to provide farm homestead units upon which men can make a living."[24] Congressman Edward Keating, a prominent Progressive from Colorado, emphatically assured his colleagues that the bill would ensure benefits to the homesteader rather than the "land-grabbing corporations."[25]

Often in this congressional debate, stockmen with large holdings were pictured as being of the same mold as the rapacious corporations. Mr. McClintic argued that such stockmen had traditionally controlled the public domain in the West, therefore preventing the "little fellow" from launching a successful beginning in the livestock business. He further condemned the large cattle interests for having taken handsome profits from their business while having had free use of public grazing lands.[26] With apparent relish, Congressman Raker of California pronounced an end to the day of the cattle kings and to their undisputed control of the public range. He suggested that the cattle interests had been unable to displace the Kinkaid homesteaders, and he expressed doubt that they would be able to consolidate sizeable tracts under the proposed bill—an opinion with which Congressman E. E. Roberts of Nevada rose in agreement.[27]

In discussing the economic opportunities of the bill, congressional proponents were lavish in their assessment of what individual owners were capable of accomplishing, even on marginal lands. Here the assumptions and expressions dovetailed with those articulated in committee hearings as well as those common to the popular literature. These new entrepreneurs, the argument ran, would bring enthusiasm, imagination, and daring to the enterprise. With these qualities, anything seemed possible. In an early debate on the measure, Congressman Fergusson advanced his familiar claim that the small farmer was more inclined than the large lessee to make improvements on the land and in the quality of livestock.[28] Congressman Edward T. Taylor had similar thoughts, adding that by using newly developed techniques and suitable crops the settler could maintain a home and family even on the most arid and rugged terrain encompassed by the bill.[29] According to Congressman McClintic, settlers who took grants under the proposed measure would soon transform "a barren desert into happy homes and thriving, prosperous communities."[30] This type of miracle had been wrought in portions of Oklahoma, he assured his colleagues, as soon as the settlers had been able to wrest control of the land from the cattlemen. Congressman Raker also lent voice to this promise, pointing to the Enlarged Homestead Act of 1909 as vindication. As he portrayed it, that act not only allowed settlers to gain homes but also channeled their energies into the building of communities, schools, and roads.[31]

The promise of economic development was the most persistent argument marshalled in support of the act. Congressman Taylor, the most eloquent of the many congressional spokesmen on this matter, quoted from a recent report of the House Committee on Public Lands, which wedded this tenet with that of commercial development of natural resources in a way that Theodore Roosevelt would have approved:

> It takes homes to insure permanent taxpayers; it takes homes to bring schools and churches; it takes homes to build cities and towns that attract and support labor and mechanics; population invites railroads, which in turn bring more immigration and capital to develop the barely touched resources of this great semiarid West.[32]

It is unclear whether Taylor envisioned the same type of development of natural resources as Roosevelt, but the similarities in rhetoric are striking.

Taylor also predicted that the act would result in the addition of thousands of new homes to each western state and would transform several million acres of previously worthless land into productive tracts that would then be added to the tax rolls. Congressman McClintic reiterated this point of view, although his estimates were more modest. Having noted that homesteaders in Oklahoma had contributed to the development of the gypsum, cement, granite, flour, and cheese industries of that state, he opined that the proposed act would "cause the undeveloped natural resources to be thoroughly investigated" in each of the newly opened areas.[33] Congressman Hernandez voiced similar thoughts. Admitting that New Mexico was in financial straits, he foresaw the grazing homestead act as a source of relief, if not deliverance. Not only would the act add new land to assessment rolls, but it would provide people to aid in the development of the state's resources.

Nearly every supporter agreed that the act would be an economic boon to the West. Such agreement need not cast cynical aspersions on the motives of the bill's proponents nor otherwise detract from their sincerity in advancing the bill. If the act were to work the wonders pictured by its supporters, its economic consequences would be profound. It is around this "if-then" proposition that the final considerations of this chapter logically revolve: the sectional alignment the bill occasioned in Congress and the place of the act in President Wilson's New Freedom.

Recall that as early as 1909 the Country Life Commission had found that the urge to move to new places in order to gain greater acreage was strong among the nation's farmers. This fact was acknowledged several times in the congressional debates. Even one of the opponents of the measure, Congressman William H. Stafford of Wisconsin, recognized that there were "large numbers of people" who desired to homestead on the public domain.[34] But after objecting to the bill on the grounds that it favored the westerner at the expense of others, Stafford was unable to respond when challenged by a colleague to explain how anyone could enter a claim under the act without going West and in fact being a westerner. It was, of course, movement from the East to the West on which the bill's western supporters based their anticipation of the development of their respective states and to which they had given such elocution. It was Mondell's opinion that 90 percent of those who moved to Wyoming under the Enlarged Homestead Act of 1909 had come from states east of the Missouri River, and he predicted similar results under the Stock Raising Homestead Act.[35] The beneficiaries of the act, in other words, would be westerners, midwesterners, southerners, and easterners alike.

Later in the debates Stafford again acknowledged those "thousands living in the Midwest" who were looking for an opportunity to gain land, but he argued that the bill would not attract those people to the West. His logic seemed confused, however, when in the next breath he stated that he would be more inclined to support the proposal if he did not feel that much land still remained suitable for homesteading under the Act of 1909.[36] (He seemed undisturbed by the fact that thousands of midwestern constituents obviously disagreed.) In the debate of the following day he effected yet another turnabout, insisting that the bill, as amended, represented a sellout to the stock barons.[37]

Although the opposition to the bill, such as it was, seems to have been centered mostly in the Midwest, at least one congressman from that section anticipated positive benefits accruing to the Midwest under the act. Congressman William P. Borland of Missouri pointed out that for some time the farmers of the Missouri and Mississippi valleys had been experiencing difficulty in raising enough young stock and feeders to capitalize fully on the fattening operations so naturally suited to those areas. According to his analysis, this was one of the primary reasons for the relative shortage of beef then available for marketing. An operation likely to be pursued on a grazing homestead would be the production of replacement stock, and large numbers of these cattle could be expected to find their way to the feedlots of the Midwest. Similar benefits would be felt in the sheep industry as well. The farmers of Missouri had a genuine need for sheep to clear pasturage and brushwood, but they were presently faced with an insufficient source of young stock to meet their demand. As Borland saw it, the grazing homesteaders of the West would provide that source.[38]

On the other hand, one western congressman was an outspoken critic of the bill, especially as it drew near a vote. Having first professed sympathy with the intent of the measure and having paid due respect to the positive effects of the Enlarged Homestead Act of 1909, Congressman Robert M. McCracken of Idaho then argued vigorously the stockmen's point of view. He voiced fear that a group of designing men could make entry on "large tracts of land" (presumably contiguous tracts) with the sole intent of obstructing the use of public grazing lands by the stockmen in order to exact tribute from them. He insisted that enactment of the bill would largely destroy Idaho's livestock industry, and he inserted in the record a statement from the Wool Growers' Association to that effect.[39]

Congressman James R. Mann of Illinois was another outspoken critic, particularly in the earlier debates; and he, Stafford, and McCracken comprised the heart of the opposition corps. But unlike McCracken, and to a great extent like Stafford, Mann was careful to keep his motives concealed. His criticism was generally confined to charges that the bill reflected poor syntax and that many of its provisions were loosely drawn. He was especially critical of the provision specifying the type of land to be open for entry, charging that the net effect was to make the bill one "under which if 639 acres will support a family, you can not get 640 acres, and under which if 641 acres are necessary to support a family, you can not get 640 acres."[40] So insistent was he that Congressman Irvine L. Lenroot of Wisconsin, though himself mildly opposed to the bill, chided him for interpreting literally that which was obviously intended as a guideline only.[41]

At a point about midway through the debates, Mann, apparently perceiving the momentum that had been generated in support of the bill, withdrew from further participation. In so doing he predicted that legislation of this type would be enacted and that "possibly it ought to be." Notwithstanding the uncertainty of the source of his opposition, the fact remains that he was the only congressman to have articulated clearly the basic economic fallacy of the act when he remarked that "no man can make a living by grazing stock on 640 acres where he can not raise anything else."[42]

There was only a small amount of debate in the Senate on the Stock Raising Homestead Act, and what little activity the bill occasioned in that chamber was generally of the procedural sort. Although passed by the House in the third session of the Sixty-third Congress (in January 1915), the bill was not taken up by the Senate prior to adjournment. It was subsequently passed again by the House early in the next session (January 1916) and again seemed to experience difficulty in gaining a hearing on the Senate floor. The bill's eventual consideration and passage by the upper house was undoubtedly influenced to a sizeable extent by the positive assistance lent by President Wilson.

The most explicit statement of Wilson's views on public resource policy conservation is in one of his campaign speeches of 1912. He charged that designing men bent on monopolistic control of the nation's resources had hitherto stood so close to government that it had feared to release the

natural resources for development. The "bona fide settler" had been ignored, and the government had locked away much of the nation's potential strength. The heart of Wilson's proposal harks back to the Progressive
view of conservation:

> The trouble about conservation is that the government of the United
> States hasn't any policy at present. It is simply marking time. It is
> simply standing still. Reservation is not conservation. Simply to say,
> "We are not going to do anything about the forests," when the country
> needs to use the forests, is not a practicable program at all. . . . There
> can't be a working program until there is a free government. The day
> when the government is free to set about a policy of positive conserva-
> tion, as distinguished from mere negative reservation, will be an emanci-
> pation day of no small importance for the development of the country.[43]

Wilson went on to ask of what value is the country's storehouse of
resources if intelligent and vigorous use of them is denied; of what value
are resources which are not developed into tangible wealth.

Wilson's views on conservation are strikingly similar to those of Theodore Roosevelt. And both men were elaborate in their praise of those who
drew their living from the soil. The only discernible difference is one of
style. According to Wilson:

> Nothing living can blossom into fruitage unless through nourishing
> stalks deep-planted in the common soil. The rose is merely the evidence
> of the vitality of the root; and the real source of its beauty, the very
> blush that it wears upon its tender cheek, comes from those silent
> sources of life that lie hidden in the chemistry of the soil. Up from that
> soil, up from the silent bosom of the earth, rise the currents of life and
> energy. Up from the common soil, up from the quiet heart of the peo-
> ple, rise joyously to-day streams of hope and determination bound to
> renew the face of the earth in glory.[44]

That Wilson lent support to the grazing homestead bill is therefore not
surprising. In an address delivered to an Indianapolis audience in January
1915, he expressed hope that Congress would soon act to "unlock the
resources of the public domain."[45] And in his third annual message to
Congress, in December 1915, he urged that "at the same time that we
safeguard and conserve the natural resources of the country we should put
them at the disposal of those who will use them promptly and intelli-
gently, as was sought to be done in the admirable bills submitted to the
last Congress from its committees on the public lands."[46]

Wilson's advice was taken. The grazing homestead bill was passed by the Senate on September 8, 1916, and the president signed it into law a few weeks later.

It happens, then, that the Stock Raising Homestead Act, as formulated and debated in congressional committee and chambers from 1914 to 1916, was a logical response to the growing back-to-the-land sentiment in the United States. The debates in Congress reveal an obvious awareness of this sentiment. The congressional rhetoric advanced in favor of the bill showed a noticeable resemblance to the back-to-the-land genre of literature. The Stock Raising Homestead Act also appears to have been a logical extension of the public land policy desired by President Wilson. It represented the principle of use and commercial development of the public domain by that bona fide settler championed so eloquently by both Wilson and Theodore Roosevelt. President Wilson clearly saw the act as consonant with the principles of conservation.

Sectional alignment occasioned in Congress by the bill was not pronounced. There was strong support for it among many western congressmen, but there was also some western opposition. Furthermore, a leasing bill, offered as the alternative to grazing homesteads, was sponsored by a Californian. Most opposition to the bill was centered in a handful of congressmen from the rich farm belt of the Midwest, but the opposition block was neither large nor well organized. At least one Missouri congressman was friendly to the measure; and if Oklahoma is considered a midwestern state, one would have to acknowledge on the basis of that delegation's support that midwestern support for the bill was at least as strong as midwestern opposition to it. The congressional debates reveal no indication of opposition from eastern or southern states.

Disillusion with Disposal

The decade of the 1920s was a pivotal one for public land policy in the United States. It began with a clear commitment to disposal of millions of acres in relatively small parcels to individual homesteaders. It ended at a crossroad, with the nation again debating the direction of the future. This time, in contrast to the debates of the teens, the issues were more closely linked to actual experience and the rhetoric was devoid of romantic allusions. It was a serious business from the outset, one that foreshadowed the sensitive nature of public resource issues that has come to characterize post-frontier America.

The first round opened in 1929. In August, at the Conference of Public Land States' Governors held in Salt Lake City, a letter from President Hoover was read which expressed his conviction that the western states could manage the administration of public lands and reclamation more competently than the federal government. He then proposed the creation of a commission to study the advisability of relinquishing the remaining public domain to the various states in which these lands were located. This proposal was a natural sequel to the notion advanced by Interior Secretary Ray Lyman Wilbur to the Conference of Western Governors the previous month when he stated his belief that "it is time for a new public land policy which will include transferring to those states willing to accept the responsibility the control of the surface rights of all public lands not included in national parks or monuments or in the national forests."[1] It might eventually develop, Secretary Wilbur hinted, that even the control of existing national forests would be best turned over to the states.

Even though there was no unanimity among the western governors in their views toward this proposal,[2] Congress authorized the creation of the commission recommended by President Hoover and appropriated funds for it in April 1930. To this Committee on the Conservation and Administration of the Public Domain were appointed twenty members representing an impressive and logical array of professional and sectional interests. James R.

Garfield, son of the former president, and himself former secretary of the interior during two years of the Roosevelt administration, was appointed chairman. Among the remaining nineteen members of the "Garfield Committee" were W. B. Greeley, secretary-manager of the West Coast Lumbermen's Association and former chief of the U.S. Forest Service; Rudolph Kuchler, president of the State Taxpayer's Association of Arizona; George H. Lorimer, editor of the *Saturday Evening Post;* Elwood Mead, commissioner of the Bureau of Reclamation; I. H. Nash, state land commissioner of Idaho; William Peterson, director of the Experiment Station and Extension Division, Utah State Agricultural College; and Francis C. Wilson, interstate river commissioner for New Mexico. In addition to the twenty members were two ex officio members: Ray Lyman Wilbur, secretary of the interior, and Arthur M. Hyde, secretary of agriculture.

That the committee was weighted heavily in favor of western interests is understandable considering that the preponderance of unreserved public land was in the western states (see table 2).

During the summer of 1930 the committee members busied themselves in personally examining large portions of the public domain, in receiving testimony from interested individuals, and in collecting editorials and other printed data valuable in the assessment of public opinion.[3] In November the committee reconvened in Washington, D.C., to collate its information and arrive at a conclusion. Its *Report,* submitted to the president in January 1931, advanced twenty specific recommendations—many of which were strictly procedural—in support of the following substantive conclusions:

1. To the public-land states should be granted all the unreserved, unappropriated public domain within their respective boundaries, conditional upon legislative acceptance, within ten years, by each state.

2. States not desiring to accept this grant of public land would have the option of requesting, by appropriate legislation within ten years, that the president, by executive order, designate these public lands as national range to be administered in the same manner as national forests.

3. In the absence of any state legislation within ten years, the president may, when authorized by Congress, designate these public lands as national range.

TABLE TWO

Area of Vacant, Unappropriated, and Unreserved Public Lands, as of June 30, 1930

State	Area, in acres		
	Surveyed	Unsurveyed	Total
Arizona	8,084,880	7,096,000	15,180,880
Arkansas	190,969	—	190,969
California	11,284,395	5,339,093	16,623,488
Colorado	6,825,425	1,202,043	8,027,468
Florida	12,245	6,652	18,897
Idaho	8,765,491	1,852,479	10,617,970
Minnesota	189,845	—	189,845
Montana	6,510,937	90,740	6,601,677
Nebraska	22,628	—	22,628
Nevada	30,064,688	21,389,805	51,454,493
New Mexico	14,316,481	1,347,640	15,664,121
North Dakota	146,505	—	146,505
Oregon	12,976,725	92,411	13,069,136
South Dakota	439,880	—	439,880
Utah	12,378,068	11,503,377	23,881,445
Washington	906,382	14,202	920,584
Wyoming	15,185,722	743,738	15,929,460
Grand Total	128,301,266	50,678,180	178,979,446

Source: U.S. Congress, Senate, *Report of the Committee on the Conservation and Administration of the Public Domain*, appended to Senate Committee on Public Lands and Surveys, *Granting Remaining Unreserved Public Lands to States, Hearings . . . on S. 17, S. 2272, and S. 4060*, 72d Cong., 1st sess., 1932, 343.

4. These public lands should be clearly listed with the Department of the Interior as to mineral or nonmineral character, that the title to both should be granted to the states in fee simple, but that in the case of the former the federal government should reserve all minerals for its permittees, lessees, or grantees to prospect for, mine, and remove.[4]

A bill embodying the proposals of the Garfield Committee was drafted by that body and printed as an appendix to the *Report*. This draft, altered slightly by James Garfield, was introduced in the Senate by Gerald P. Nye of North Dakota and in the House by John M. Evans of Montana. A similar bill was also introduced at that time by Senator Walsh of Montana, differing from the Nye-Evans measure to the extent of including the mineral rights in the proposed grant of unreserved, unappropriated public lands to the states. Hearings on these measures were held before the House Committee on Public Lands and the Senate Committee on Public Lands and Surveys during the early months of 1932. Neither bill survived those hearings. In fact, the repudiation of the disposal concept was so emphatic that within two more years the federal government would finally initiate a grazing regulation program that represented the very antithesis of the Nye-Evans bill. The Taylor Grazing Act of 1934 signaled the death knell to homesteading and other plans to parcel out the public domain to state or individual ownership. Henceforth, the federal government would be not just the owner of public lands but a proprietor, not just an absentee landlord looking for a buyer but an aggressive manager of this vast acreage.

Why the sudden turnabout? How could president and Congress have moved so abruptly from such an apparently popular and traditionally American position as homesteading toward a posture of tightfisted ownership? The answer lies in a convergence of social, economic, demographic, climatic, and ecological considerations that burst upon the national consciousness in 1930. Much of the story belongs to the twentieth-century homesteaders, much to the grazing stockmen, and not a little to the unique topography of the semiarid American West.

Despite genuine effort from a large number of dry-farm homesteaders, the Enlarged Homestead Act of 1909 did not begin to measure up to the hopes and expectations of its sponsors. Its best success came on the northern Great Plains where thousands of homesteaders moved into the western Dakotas and eastern Montana to try their hand at this new system of agriculture. Generally inattentive to the little technical literature available on the subject, they proceeded by trial and error, guided by a basic optimism and, in many cases, previous experience as farmers in the subhumid regions of the Midwest.[5]

In 1910, the first full year of operation for the Enlarged Homestead Act, nearly 22,000 people entered claims in the Dakotas and Montana alone. Some were speculators; they tended to locate in districts served by railroads and were less concerned about the quality of land. Most, however, were genuinely interested in dry-land farming and they worked hard at it. Initially beset by drought and inexperience, they nevertheless enjoyed good weather and higher grain prices during the war years. Then came a series of droughts and tumbling prices beginning in the late teens and extending through the 1920s. Few homesteaders could cope with such a combination for long, and most of them sold or abandoned their claims.[6]

Within the Rocky Mountain region, dry farming enjoyed its best success in the northern Utah–southern Idaho area. Utah, of course, had seen extensive dry farming since the 1860s as the Mormons had experimented with dry-farm crops and techniques from Juab County on the south to Cache County on the north. By 1895 some 34,627 acres were under dry-farm agriculture in Cache County alone; Box Elder, Davis, and Utah counties each boasted over 10,000 dry-farm acres. Though of a lesser magnitude in Idaho, dry farming was nevertheless visible on lands in Gentile and Malad valleys by the 1890s.[7]

Utah had the advantage not only of experience but also of the vision and enthusiasm of John A. Widtsoe. As a professor of agronomy at Utah State Agricultural College and director of the Utah Experiment Station, he lobbied successfully with the state's governor and legislature to fund the establishment of five experimental farms in 1903, and from this base he promoted the concept of dry farming throughout the state. In addition to his previously mentioned book, *Dry-Farming: A System of Agriculture for Countries Under a Low Rainfall,* Widtsoe authored numerous articles and reports. He traveled extensively throughout the region to spread the dry-farming gospel; and, in a joint effort with colleague Lew Merrill, even put together a special two-car train, the Farmers' Institute Special, that took a two-week tour through Utah and Idaho in 1909 and 1910, carrying speakers, pamphlets, and exhibitions in support of dry farming.[8]

Perhaps because of the early advances in Utah dry farming, the Enlarged Homestead Act did not have a great impact on the area. However, hundreds of thousands of Utah and Idaho acres were classified for entry under the act and many homesteaders did take advantage of the opportunity. Matthew Bird entered a claim in the Arbon Valley of southern Idaho, for example, and recorded in his diary that "the whole valley was alive with new farmers." Bird succeeded, as did many others; but those who entered on marginal lands were not so lucky, particularly during the years of economic recession following the war.[9] In this respect, the Utah-Idaho experience was similar to the Dakotas and Montana. It was different in that the Enlarged Homestead Act prompted no significant population boom in Utah and southern Idaho. Most who took out claims were locals merely seeking to add acreage to existing farms.

Elsewhere in the West, success was spotty at best. The Dry Farm Homestead Act triggered a rush of homesteaders to northeastern Colorado—most of them second- and third-generation European immigrants from Iowa, Nebraska, and other midwestern states. Many of them lived in tents until they had the time and money to build houses. They generally enjoyed success during the early years but, in keeping with the larger western pattern, fell victim to falling grain prices after the war and to drought cycles in the 1920s and early 1930s. [10]

In Wyoming, the boom-bust cycle was of even shorter duration. Its dry-farming region, located in the southeast portion of the state, experienced a roller-coaster profile of activity, with a rush of dry farmers in 1909 and 1910, followed by drought and abandonments in 1911, then more settlement activity from 1912 to 1914. The scale of immigration was never large, however, despite some intensive promotional efforts by the Board of Immigration and various private interests. [11]

Nevada's experience would have been even less gratifying to the sponsors of the Enlarged Homestead Act. A brief flurry of settlement activity, particularly in Elko County, followed the act. The communities of Metropolis, northwest of Wells, and Tobar, southeast of Wells, sprang into existence as dry-farm homesteaders, mostly from Utah, took their optimism and dreams into those valleys. In 1909 the state legislature did its part to promote the idea by appropriating funds for the establishment of an experimental dry farm in Pleasant Valley, near Tobar. But little success was achieved. Dry years from the outset, jackrabbit invasions, and exceptionally harsh winters combined to frustrate even the hardiest dry-farm homesteaders. By 1917 most of them were gone, and the state closed its experimental farm. [12]

The same blush of optimism and activity that immediately followed the Enlarged Homestead Act also attended the Stock Raising Homestead Act. By 1923, for example, over six million acres of land on the northern Great Plains was entered for grazing homesteads. During the peak years from 1919 to 1923, over thirty-five million acres throughout the West were entered under the act. By 1934 the total number of acres approached sixty million. [13]

Yet, even more completely than the Enlarged Homestead Act, the Stock Raising Homestead Act failed to measure up to the rhetoric of its sponsors and other supporters. Less than half the original entries were ever carried to final patent. The act simply had no economic feasibility to it. In a detailed 1918 study of grazing conditions in Arizona, USGS engineer E. C. La Rue determined that where 20 to 150 acres of land were required to support one cow, as in Arizona, then from 3,000 to 22,500 acres would be required to support a livestock-raising family. Conditions were not greatly different in Utah—where the average carrying capacity of public grazing land was sufficient for only one cow per 15 acres—or elsewhere in the Mountain West. A single section of this kind of land, which in many cases could support only about forty cows, was hopelessly inadequate.[14]

Naturally, in the absence of economic viability, homesteaders were destined to disappointment in terms of quality-of-life considerations. The rhapsodic promises of Congressman Church and the romantic visions of Congressman McClintic eventually reverberated as sour notes in the actual homesteading score. In 1925, Will C. Barnes, assistant forester and chief of grazing for the U.S. Forest Service, summed up the enlarged homesteading experience on the recalcitrant western lands in these terms:

> Eager citizens have combed these areas over and over and have cut the very heart out of them in search of a piece of land upon which they could locate, produce agricultural crops, and make a home for themselves and families. It is not there to-day. They recalled the stories of their fathers and grandfathers of the rich lands once open to settlement in States like Iowa, Illinois, and the Dakotas. They found instead only an arid climate, lands more or less infested with alkali and other injurious elements, no water for irrigation except at costs now wholly prohibitive, and surroundings generally inhospitable and unattractive.[15]

Barnes described one group of stock-raising homesteaders west of Taos, New Mexico, as he had observed them in 1922. Situated in rugged, semiarid terrain, they were forced to spend an inordinate amount of time and effort hauling water to their homesteads—up to ten miles over primitive roads. Most of them were veterans and young men and women from surrounding communities. They were teachers, clerks, and other city-oriented people. Very few of them were experienced with livestock, and almost none of them intended to make a permanent home on their entries. Barnes noted similar conditions in Montana and Wyoming. The water situation was better but, like the New Mexico group, "one and all were looking for some stockmen to come along and buy them out."[16]

But the grazing stockmen also faced difficult times in the 1920s. In addition to the problem of generally depressed market conditions, they also found the carrying capacity of the unappropriated public grazing lands to be diminishing each year. Ranges became increasingly crowded and denuded. On such ranges as the West Desert of Utah, transient herders moved their stock at will, disregarding the time-honored, unwritten agreements among the old-time outfits on territorial rights.[17] Stockmen became ever more fidgety as their losses mounted.

Actually, the ranges had been deteriorating for years. Forest reserves were so badly overgrazed when Gifford Pinchot became chief forester, for example, that he took radical steps—including the initiation of grazing fees—to halt further destruction. Although originally resisted by the stockmen, these measures proved effective enough in restoring the forest grazing lands that by 1914, despite their perpetual complaints about the cost of grazing permits, most western cattlemen and sheepmen favored the Kent bill over the stock raising homestead proposal.

In large part due to agitation from stockmen, over a dozen grazing bills were introduced into Congress between 1906 and 1924. None of them saw enactment; on only two were hearings even held. While the stockmen shared a consensus that something should be done, they could not agree on particulars. This, along with the traditional rivalry between the agriculture and interior departments, served to thwart final congressional action during those years.[18]

In the meantime, the public ranges continued to deteriorate. Will C. Barnes, writing in 1925, announced that the public domain was "so badly overgrazed as to be more of a liability than an asset."[19] He also included a number of revealing photographs with his report, which report was incorporated into congressional hearings on the matter in 1925. Other testimony at those hearings corroborated Barnes's dire view. Still, nothing was done.

Even the two spectacular Utah flash floods of August 13, 1923, failed to convey a proper warning. One, in Willard, took two lives; the other, in Farmington, claimed seven. The latter was particularly dramatic as the lethal torrent cascaded from the mouth of Farmington Canyon, caught six unsuspecting campers in its wake, and carried them to a grisly death. Four were boy scouts. The other two, Walter Wright and his wife Wealtha, were from Farmington. The force of the torrent severed the pregnant wife at the waist. The six bodies were not recovered from the muck and debris until two days later.[20] Apparently, officials thought that such a freakish occurrence was a capricious act of nature—something that would never recur. Neglect continued apace throughout the remainder of the decade.

But in 1930, just as the Garfield Committee was at its busiest, climatic events in Utah initiated a renewed public awareness of the fragile nature of public grazing lands. The drought of that year ended abruptly in the northern part of the state on July 10. For a number of farmers along the Wasatch Front—those in the Centerville and Farmington areas of Davis County—relief quickly turned to alarm as they watched a cloudburst discharge against the steep mountainside bordering their farmlands on the east. In a matter of minutes a crest of water ten feet high roared out of an adjacent canyon. It descended upon the home of Eugene and Joseph Ford, razed it, struck the side of their hay-filled barn, swept it forward several rods, and then demolished it. A coop containing two hundred chickens on the David F. Smith farm, and one containing seventeen hundred chickens on a neighboring farm, were also swept away. Thirty-five sheep on the Ernest Burnham farm were destroyed. As the crest rushed westward it left a large portion of the Hiram Ford farm covered with a layer of silt up to four feet deep, washed out a five-hundred-foot strip of the state highway, and left a deposit of silt a foot deep in the area. A few miles north, in Weber Canyon, another cloudburst washed an estimated quarter of a million tons of debris into the canyon, obliterating large areas of the highway and the Union Pacific tracks by leaving a pile of boulders as deep as thirty-five feet in places. The storm exacted an estimated one million dollars in property damage, but miraculously, no loss of life.[21]

A month later, during the afternoon of August 11, 1930, a second cloudburst unleashed its fury against the barren mountainside east of Centerville and Farmington. Almost immediately a torrent of destruction, described by one observer as "a mass of chocolate-colored waters, about the consistency of a heavy paint," rushed from Parrish, Ford, Davis, and Steed canyons down on the two communities below. Acres of fruit trees were uprooted and carried forward.

The home and outbuildings of Herbert Streeper were demolished as were the outbuildings and two rooms of the home of Henry Barber. State Senator David F. Smith lost his home, outbuildings, and six hundred chickens. Several other homes and buildings were either destroyed or badly damaged, and at least a dozen cows were swept away. Nearly a mile of the public highway was left covered with a layer of debris ten feet deep, and an estimated twenty thousand dollars' worth of crops were destroyed. Although eighty-year-old Charles Hughes was carried nearly two hundred yards by the tide and was left buried to his neck in muck, neither he nor any other person lost his life. But approximately a hundred acres of Utah's choicest farm land was ravaged.[22]

That was Monday. On Wednesday the bottom again dropped from the clouds and again the hideous reverberations from the mountains signalled the rush of more muck and destruction from the canyons—this time from seven of them, ranging from Beck's in north Salt Lake City to Sheppard, north of Farmington. Four more houses, several more outbuildings, additional strips of highway, railroad tracks, fields, and orchards fell to the juggernaut. Again, Centerville was hardest hit. A survey of the area on the following day disclosed that twenty-six families had suffered from the recent disasters and 175 acres of farmland, valued at a thousand dollars per acre, had been cleared of crops. Individual losses ranged from five to fifty thousand dollars.[23]

Though the Centerville and Farmington areas experienced the greatest devastation, many areas of the state suffered from the August runoff. They included Bingham Canyon and Magna, just west of Salt Lake City; Ophir Canyon in Tooele County; and the Utah County communities of Provo, Springville, and Pleasant Grove. Less severe floods were experienced farther south—in the areas of Moroni, Silver City, Panguitch, Orangeville, and in Grand and San Juan counties.

Following the August 13 flood, Governor George H. Dern announced that he was ordering a survey of the Davis County area to determine the causes of the recent floods and to prevent or minimize future ones. He was personally persuaded that overgrazing by sheep was the primary cause, and he publicly said so. The *Salt Lake Tribune* editorialized similarly and featured a number of letters to the editor charging overgrazing and poor management as the obvious cause of the floods.[24]

During the night of September 4, 1930, the fourth storm of the summer, only slightly less severe than the previous three, again sent torrents of waterborne soil, boulders, and vegetation down on the battered homes and farms of Centerville and Farmington. Most of the progress that had been made in reclamation was negated in a matter of minutes, and the farmers emerged disconsolate from their night of terror. W. W. Parrish of Centerville, upon observing that the storm had covered with debris the land he had spent a month clearing, reported: "I'm going to leave it that way now, unless they do something to reforest the hills and give us a chance." Several of his neighbors expressed similar sentiments.[25]

By September 9 Governor Dern had created and staffed the Flood Commission composed of stockmen, geologists, engineers, bankers, range managers, and conservationists. On December 31 it transmitted its report to the governor, who immediately directed publication.

The causes of the many floods throughout the state, according to the report, were (1) uncommonly heavy rainfall, (2) steep topography, and especially (3) scant vegetation on the watersheds. "There is ample evidence on the watersheds of Davis County," the commissioners asserted, "to show that had the plant cover been approximately equal to its original natural condition, the flooding in that section from the rains of 1930 would have been far less serious, if not prevented."[26]

On the causes of denudation, the report was very explicit. Excessive cutting of timber had been a contributory cause, as were fires. But the primary cause of depletion was overgrazing. The commissioners' investigation disclosed that even the vegetation normally unpalatable to livestock had been largely depleted before the end of July 1930. At the watering places and in the more favorable grazing places, the ground was almost bare. Overgrazing had been done by both sheep and cattle, the former on the steeper slopes, the latter on the gentler ones.

The commission then turned to the crucial matter of preventive maintenance, and its recommendations were sweeping. Most crucial was the acquisition of all critical watershed areas by the state or federal government. The commission also recommended that grazing be prohibited on the heads of several of the canyons until plant cover had been restored, that a vigorous reforestation program be launched immediately, and that an effective fire prevention and suppression program be established.

The commission also advanced a program of watershed protection for the three million acres of highly important watershed lands elsewhere in the state that were presently being neglected for want of state or public administrative attention.

Governor Dern was impressed with the report of the Flood Commission. He publicly said he was, and he used the report as the basis for additional research and thought. By the time of the hearings on the Nye-Evans bill a year later, he was firmly opposed to any cession of public lands. In the extensive hearings on that measure,[27] the charismatic Dern became something of a star witness. He spent several days before the House Committee on Public Lands in February 1931 and spoke with a confidence that came not only from being well versed but also from the realization that he represented a virtually unanimous constituency.[28]

Special interests elsewhere were not nearly as united in their views on the cession proposal. A number of them favored it, such as the Wyoming Woolgrowers and the American National Livestock Association. A number also opposed it, such as the State Woolgrowers of Colorado, the Idaho

Woolgrower's Association, and the American Farm Bureau Federation. Among the western governors, some supported cession, others were opposed, and still others remained silent. But the majority took Utah's lead and cession was soundly defeated.

In summary, several events and circumstances came together in 1930 to reverse public land policy. First, enlarged homesteading, that is, 320- and 640-acre parcels, was generally a failure, in large measure because little public land suitable for homesteading remained after the turn of the century. Second, many years of overgrazing and undermanagement of the unappropriated public domain had badly depleted what viable land there was. Third, President Hoover opened the entire matter to public debate with his proposal of late 1929 to relinquish federal ownership of remaining public lands. And fourth, a series of expensive and spectacular floods along the populated region of the Wasatch Front commanded congressional attention and fixed the commitment of Utah's governor and congressional delegation in support of aggressive federal management of the public domain.

Professor Gates reminds us that Congressman Edward T. Taylor of Colorado "has a special niche in history because he was the man who finally maneuvered through the House both the 640-acre Stock Raising Homestead Act in 1916 and later the Grazing Act of 1934, which took his name and in effect reversed the earlier act, which he had come to regret."[29] But the Taylor Grazing Act was really the brainchild of Don B. Colton, congressman from Utah. Had Colton maintained his seat in Congress, perhaps the grazing act would have carried his name. Regardless, the great shift in public land policy—away from disposal and toward strong federal management—cut across party and sectional lines. It was driven not by theory or transitory ideology but by telling experience registered over a considerable period of time.

The Taylor Grazing Act of 1934 ended forever the fantasy of free public lands and the hope of someday "proving up" on a picturesque homestead nestled in an imagined valley at the base of the Rockies. The national infatuation with free land, along with optimism in the individual's ability to reclaim semiarid lands, withered and died under the harsh realities of actual experience—experience that proved that the fragile but intractable western lands are better at stimulating dreams than sustaining them.

Epilogue

The Taylor Grazing Act of 1934 did not immediately end all homesteading on the public domain. Instead, it provided for the protection of preexisting rights and for the consummation of certain phase-down procedures. Still, by early 1935 homesteading had slowed to a trickle. For practical purposes, it was a thing of the past.

Even though the Taylor Act superseded the various homestead laws, including the Stock Raising Homestead Act that he had advocated so eloquently, Congressman Taylor had no doubt about its wisdom. In June 1935 he publicly lamented the "tragic loss" of money and labor as well as the "appalling hardships and heartbreaking disappointments" experienced by twentieth-century homesteaders. He apparently felt no embarrassment over his turnabout, and indeed he need not have. His was an empirical response based on eighteen years of observation. By 1934 he, along with millions of other Americans, could see the folly of enlarged homesteading. In advocating its supersession he was simply articulating a national consensus.

That consensus has held remarkably firm from that time to this. Federal ownership and management of the public domain is well accepted and generally appreciated by the majority of citizens. Periodic attempts by special interests to effect transfer of public lands to the states—the most notable being those of the late 1940s and the late 1970s—have never really fired the public imagination or developed a significant political base.

The latter effort, the so-called Sagebrush Rebellion, is particularly instructive. Despite its catchy label and the backing of several western politicians, it held little appeal for the larger public. As with the Hoover proposal of fifty years earlier, this cession attempt was not advocated by a majority of western voices, was in fact strongly opposed by conservation interests, and got nowhere in Congress. There were differences as well. The debate of 1979–80 was not as comprehensive as it had been for the Hoover proposal, generally seemed to ignore the interstate nature of watershed management, and galvanized opposition from sportsmen and other well-organized recreation-oriented groups.

As our society continues to grow in size, urbanization, and industrialization, the average American citizen clings ever more tenaciously to his minuscule share of ownership in the public lands. For him, common ownership is preferable to no ownership. Accordingly, the general direction of public-land policy seems set for a long time to come.

Notes

INTRODUCTION

1. Benjamin H. Hibbard, *A History of the Public Land Policies* (New York: Macmillan Co., 1924), 481.

2. Everett Dick, *The Lure of the Land: A Social History of the Public Lands from the Articles of Confederation to the New Deal* (Lincoln: University of Nebraska Press, 1970), 306.

3. E. Louise Peffer, *The Closing of the Public Domain: Disposal and Reservation Policies, 1900–50* (Stanford: Stanford University Press, 1951), 166–68.

4. Paul W. Gates, *History of Public Land Law Development* (Washington, D.C.: Government Printing Office, 1968), 512.

CHAPTER ONE: THE COUNTRY-LIFE MOVEMENT

1. Commission on Country Life, *Report of the Commission on Country Life* (New York: Sturgis & Walton Co., 1917), 9–10. In his letter transmitting the report to the U.S. Senate, dated February 9, 1909, President Roosevelt expressed the same thoughts in only slightly less explicit terms. See U.S. Congress, Senate, *Report of the Commission on Country Life,* 60th Cong., 2d sess., 1909, S. Doc. 705, 6.

2. As a refresher one could not do better than to consult Roosevelt's own account in *An Autobiography* (New York: Charles Scribner's Sons, 1926), 93–128.

3. Ibid., 413–14.

4. Ibid., 413. See also Gifford Pinchot, *Breaking New Ground* (New York: Harcourt, Brace and Co., 1947), 340–44.

5. *Report of the Commission on Country Life,* 25.

6. Despite the wide historiographical divergence on the definition of a Progressive, Gifford Pinchot seems to enjoy that status by acclamation. Bailey and

Butterfield are identified as Progressives on the basis that the political views that they did express, on such basic domestic issues as conservation, restraint of trade, and rural revitalization, coincided almost exactly with those of Theodore Roosevelt. Page's identification as a Progressive should be virtually uncontested. *World's Work* reflected a thoroughgoing Rooseveltian orientation on nearly every political issue.

7. *Report of the Commission on Country Life,* 14.

8. Ibid., 37.

9. Ibid., 22.

10. Ibid., 23.

11. *The Country Life Movement in the United States* (New York: Macmillan Co., 1911), 5, 61.

12. Ibid., 4–5.

13. Ibid., 1–2.

14. Ibid., 19–20.

15. Ibid., 16.

16. Kenyon L. Butterfield, *The Farmer and the New Day* (New York: Macmillan Co., 1919), 233.

17. Ibid., 8–9.

18. "Better Farming, Better Business, Better Living," *The Outlook,* February 19, 1910, 398.

19. "The Neglected Farmer," *The Outlook,* February 5, 1910, 302.

20. Ibid., 299.

21. "Better Farming," 397.

22. G. Walter Fiske, *The Challenge of the Country: A Study of Country Life Opportunity* (New York: Association Press, 1912), xii.

23. Ibid., 35.

24. Lyman Beecher Stowe, "Training City Boys for Country Life," *The Outlook,* November 9, 1912, 537.

25. Ibid., November 16, 1912, 586.

26. Ibid., 588–91.

27. Ibid., November 9, 1912, 537.

28. Ibid., November 16, 1912, 591.

29. Roosevelt, *Autobiography,* 416.

CHAPTER TWO: THE POLITICS OF THE ENLARGED HOMESTEAD ACT

1. *An Act to Provide for an Enlarged Homestead, Statutes at Large,* 35, 639–40 (1909). For a concise account of the provisions of the Enlarged Homestead Act, see Gates, *History of Public Land Law Development,* 503–9.

2. Commission on Country Life, *Report of the Commission on Country Life* (New York: Sturgis & Walton Co., 1917), 31.

3. Ibid., 34.

4. Ibid., 49.

5. "The Welfare of the Farmer," *The Outlook,* April 20, 1912, 853. Essential reading in this regard is Samuel P. Hays, *Conservation and the Gospel of Efficiency: The Progressive Conservation Movement, 1890–1920* (Cambridge: Harvard University Press, 1959).

6. Theodore Roosevelt, *An Autobiography* (New York: Charles Scribner's Sons, 1926), 94.

7. "The Welfare of the Farmer," 853.

8. "Progressive Democracy: Country Life and Conservation," *The Outlook,* September 7, 1912, 21.

9. Roosevelt, *Autobiography,* 398.

10. Mary W. M. Hargreaves, "Dry Farming Alias Scientific Farming," *Agricultural History* 22 (January 1948): 39–56.

11. Ibid., 47.

12. Ibid.

13. Ibid.

14. Ibid., 50.

15. John A. Widtsoe, *Dry-Farming: A System of Agriculture for Countries Under a Low Rainfall* (New York: Macmillan Co., 1911). For Widtsoe's assessment of Campbell, see 361–65.

16. Ibid., 413.

17. Ibid., 373–74, 412, 416.

18. Ibid., 403–6. While the actual dollar gain seems modest by today's standards, the net gain computes to an average annual increase of 7.46 percent. This would have been quite an impressive gain during that period, especially considering the economic recession of the early 1890s.

19. "Treatment of Arid Soils Discussed," *Salt Lake Tribune,* February 25, 1909, 1.

20. "Dry Farm Experts Holding Congress," *Salt Lake Tribune,* February 25, 1909, 1.

21. Ibid.

22. "Pinchot Seeks to Set Himself Right," *Salt Lake Tribune,* March 4, 1909, 1.

23. "Dry Farming Has Greatly Advanced," *Salt Lake Tribune,* March 4, 1909, 4.

24. April 1, 1908, *Congressional Record,* 60th Cong., 1st sess., 4215.

25. Ibid., 4218.

26. Ibid., April 15, 1908, 4402.

27. Ibid., 4767.

28. Ibid., May 18, 1908, 6459.

29. U.S. Congress, House, Committee on Public Lands, *To Provide for an Enlarged Homestead: Report to Accompany S.6155,* 60th Cong., 1st sess., 1908, H. Rept. 1513, 8. See also May 11, 1908, *Congressional Record,* 60th Cong., 1st sess., 6093.

30. May 11, 1908, *Congressional Record,* 60th Cong., 1st sess., 6093.

31. Ibid., 6097.

32. Ibid., 6093.

33. Ibid.

34. Ibid., 6096.

35. "Enlarged Homestead Law," *Salt Lake Tribune,* March 7, 1909, 6.

36. May 18, 1908, *Congressional Record,* 60th cong., 1st sess., 6459.

37. Typescript copy of the Reed Smoot *Diaries,* edited by Merlo Pusey, on file at the University of Utah Press, Salt Lake City.

38. "Fierce Attack on Forestry Bureau," *Salt Lake Tribune,* February 27, 1909, 1.

CHAPTER THREE: THE BACK-TO-THE-LAND MOVEMENT

1. "Land Lotteries and Land Hunger," *The Outlook,* November 29, 1913, 685.

2. "Finding a Country Home," *Collier's,* March 12, 1910, 16.

3. Ibid., 17.

4. Ernest Russell, "Taking the Plunge," *Collier's,* March 11, 1911, 16.

5. Ibid.

6. Susannah J. Keeney, "Wayback," *The Independent,* July 24, 1913, 202–4.

7. *Country Life in America, A Magazine for the Home-Maker in the Country,* March 1, 1911, cdxxxiv.

8. L. H. Bailey, "The Land Movement," *Country Life in America,* March 15, 1911, 379.

9. Grayson's various articles, all reflecting the same thesis, appeared in a number of periodicals during the second decade of the twentieth century. He was a monthly contributor to *The American Magazine* during the period 1916–17.

10. David Grayson, "The Philosophy of Soil," *Country Life in America,* March 15, 1911, 387.

11. William B. Hunter, "How Cooperation Helped Four City Business Men and Their Families to Establish Ideal Country Homes in Georgia," *Country Life in America,* 396.

12. "Back to the Farm on Fifty Dollars: An Autobiography," *Sunset,* April 1913, 362–67.

13. Ibid., 366.

14. Ibid., 367.

15. H. Gard, "The Farm Boy Who Went Back," *World's Work,* September 1910, 13445–49.

16. "Unreckoned Values in Country Living," *Collier's,* April 16, 1910, 20–21.

17. Ewing Galloway and R. H. Moulton, "The Agricultural Revolution," *Collier's,* July 26, 1913, 19–20, 28.

18. John S. Collier, quoted in "Agricultural Revolution," 20.

19. Reverend William Justin Harsha, "A Clergyman's Gamble with Uncle Sam," *The Outlook,* January 3, 1917, 24–29.

20. Ibid., 29.

21. Arthur Markley Judy, "From the Study to the Farm: A Personal Experience," *Atlantic Monthly,* May 1915, 600–613.

22. Ibid., 607–8.

23. Mabel Lewis Stuart, "The Lady Honyocker: How Girls Take Up Claims and Make Their Own Homes on the Prairie," *The Independent,* July 17, 1913, 133–37.

24. Ibid., 135.

25. Mary Isabel Brush, "Women on the Prairies: Pioneers Who Win Independence and Freedom in their One-Room Homes," *Collier's,* January 28, 1911, 17.

26. Ibid., 16.

27. Metta M. Loomis, "From a School Room to a Montana Ranch," *Overland Monthly,* January 1916, 59–64.

28. Ibid., 64.

29. Elinore Rupert, "Letters of a Woman Homesteader," *Atlantic Monthly,* October 1913, 433–43; November 1913, 589–98; December 1913, 820–30; January 1914, 17–26; February 1914, 170–77; April 1914, 525–32. These letters were

promptly published by Houghton Mifflin in 1914. In 1961 the University of Nebraska Press published them in a Bison Book edition, retaining the original title, *Letters of a Woman Homesteader*.

30. Anna W. Case, "Experiences in Locating a Home on Public Lands in the West," *Overland Monthly*, February 1918, 159–64; March 1918, 257–62.

31. Ibid., March 1918, 258–59.

CHAPTER FOUR: THE POLITICS OF THE STOCK RAISING HOMESTEAD ACT

1. *An Act to Provide for Stock-raising Homesteads, United States Statutes at Large*, Part 1, 862–65 (1916).

2. Paul W. Gates, *History of Public Land Law Development* (Washington, D.C.: Government Printing Office, 1968), 512–19.

3. U.S. Congress, House, Committee on Public Lands, *Grazing Homesteads and the Regulation of Grazing on the Public Lands. Hearings . . . on H. R. 9582 and H. R. 10539*, 63d Cong., 2d sess., 1914, 377–434.

4. Ibid., 385.

5. Ibid., 446.

6. Ibid., 460. Data later introduced into the *Hearings* showed that Jones's estimate was more nearly correct than Church's. Those data, prepared by the Department of the Interior, disclosed that the number of homestead filings for fiscal year 1912 had been 66,434; for fiscal year 1913, 76,303; and for the first six months of 1914, 36,765. See ibid., 476.

7. Ibid., 479–80.

8. Ibid., 462.

9. Ibid., 334.

10. Ibid., 438.

11. January 15, 1916, *Congressional Record*, 64th Cong., 1st sess., 1130.

12. Ibid., 1127.

13. January 18, 1915, *Congressional Record*, 63d Cong., 3d sess., 1810.

14. Ibid., 1808.

15. January 15, 1916, *Congressional Record*, 64th Cong., 1st sess., 1130.

16. Ibid.

17. January 18, 1915, *Congressional Record*, 64th Cong., 1st sess., 1225.

18. January 15, 1916, *Congressional Record*, 64th Cong., 1st sess., 1127.

19. U.S. Congress, House, Committee on Public Lands, *To Provide for Stock-raising Homesteads*, 63d Cong., 2d sess., 1914, H. Rept. 626, 11.

20. January 15, 1916, *Congressional Record,* 64th Cong., 1st sess., 1127.

21. Ibid., 1128.

22. January 17, 1916, *Congressional Record,* 64th Cong., 1st sess., 1173.

23. January 18, 1915, *Congressional Record,* 63d Cong., 3d sess., 1810.

24. Ibid., 1811.

25. January 15, 1916, *Congressional Record,* 64th Cong., 1st sess., 1130.

26. Ibid., 1127.

27. January 17, 1916, *Congressional Record,* 64th Cong., 1st sess., 1169–70.

28. January 18, 1915, *Congressional Record,* 63d Cong., 3d sess., 1807.

29. January 15, 1916, *Congressional Record,* 64th Cong., 1st sess., 1126.

30. Ibid., 1128.

31. January 17, 1916, *Congressional Record,* 64th Cong., 1st sess., 1169.

32. January 15, 1916, *Congressional Record,* 64th Cong., 1st sess., 1127.

33. Ibid., 1127–28.

34. January 18, 1915, *Congressional Record,* 63d Cong., 3d sess., 1809.

35. January 17, 1916, *Congressional Record,* 64th Cong., 1st sess., 1174.

36. Ibid.

37. January 15, 1916, *Congressional Record,* 64th Cong., 1st sess., 1221. Although Stafford was consistently opposed to the bill, he was especially vigorous in opposing the amendment which provided that a person who had previously entered a 160-acre homestead on the type of land described in the bill would be eligible to enter an additional 480 acres of that same type land, thus bringing his total entry to 640 acres.

38. January 17, 1916, *Congressional Record,* 64th Cong., 1st sess., 1173.

39. Ibid., 1174–75.

40. June 15, 1914, *Congressional Record,* 63d Cong., 2d sess., 10509.

41. January 18, 1915, *Congressional Record,* 63d Cong., 3d sess., 1812.

42. January 17, 1916, *Congressional Record,* 64th Cong., 1st sess., 1177.

43. Woodrow Wilson, *The New Freedom: A Call for the Emancipation of the Generous Energies of a People,* ed. William E. Leuchtenburg (Englewood Cliffs, N.J.: Prentice-Hall, Inc., 1961), 159.

44. Ibid., 63.

45. Albert Shaw, ed., *The Messages and Papers of Woodrow Wilson* (New York: The Review of Reviews Corporation, 1924), 86.

46. December 7, 1915, *Congressional Record,* 64th Cong., 1st sess., 99.

CHAPTER FIVE: DISILLUSION WITH DISPOSAL

1. Quoted in E. Louise Peffer, *The Closing of the Public Domain: Disposal and Reservation Policies, 1900–50* (Stanford: Stanford University Press, 1951), 203.

2. Peffer observes of the western governors: "Instead of accepting the idea with acclaim, they were inclined to view it dubiously." Ibid., 205. Roy M. Robbins, on the other hand, has asserted: "Generally speaking, the governors of the western states applauded the move, but the Senators and Representatives were not impressed." See *Our Landed Heritage: The Public Domain, 1776–1936* (Princeton: Princeton University Press, 1942), 413.

3. According to Peffer, the purpose of the committee was "to assess and evaluate public sentiment, not to create it." Her research has led her to the conclusion that the committee was not true to its calling. See *Closing of the Public Domain*, 204ff.

4. U.S. Congress, Senate, *Report of the Committee on the Conservation and Administration of the Public Domain*, appended to Senate Committee on Public Lands and Surveys, *Granting Remaining Unreserved Public Lands to States, Hearings . . . on S. 17, S. 2272, and S. 4060,* 72d Cong., 1st sess., 1932, 336–42.

5. Jeffrey B. Roet, "Agricultural Settlement on the Dry Farming Frontier, 1900–1920" (Ph.D. diss., Northwestern University, 1982), 47, 103, 135–44.

6. Ibid., 47, 98–101.

7. John Edwin Lamborn, "A History of the Development of Dry-Farming in Utah and Southern Idaho" (Master's thesis, Utah State University, 1978), 39–44.

8. Ibid., 54–56, 75–81.

9. Ibid., 111–13, 133.

10. Kathryn Nelson, *Grassland Women* (n.p.: Denver Audubon Society, Pawnee Historical Society, and Colorado Humanities Program, 1982, video cassette).

11. T. A. Larson, *History of Wyoming* (Lincoln: University of Nebraska Press, 1965), 360–65.

12. Marshall E. Bowen, "Elko County's Dry Farming Experimental Station," *Northeastern Nevada Historical Society Quarterly* 79 (Spring 1979): 35–41, 48–49. Bertie Bake, "The History of My Home Town [Metropolis]" (Reno: Nevada Federation of Womens' Clubs Records, Nevada Historical Society, 1930, typescript), 1–3.

13. Roet, "Agricultural Settlement," 40; Benjamin H. Hibbard, *A History of the Public Land Policies* (New York: Macmillan Co., 1924), 402; Paul W. Gates, *History of Public Land Law Development* (Washington, D.C.: Government Printing Office, 1968), 520.

14. "The Live Stock Industry and Grazing Conditions in Arizona," MS 75582,

pp. 146–49, Arizona Department of Library, Archives, and Public Records, Phoenix, Arizona; Gates, *History of Public Land Law Development*, 522.

15. U.S. Congress, Senate, *The Story of the Range,* quoted in *Hearings Before the Subcommittee of the Committee on Public Lands and Surveys, Pursuant to S. Res. 347 to Investigate All Matters Relating to National Forests,* 69th Cong., 1st sess., 1925, 1580.

16. Ibid., 1629.

17. Ibid., 1602.

18. Ibid., 1629–33.

19. Ibid., 1592.

20. "Nine Die in Floods in Northern Utah Towns," *Salt Lake Tribune,* August 15, 1923, 1; "Ready Response to State's Call for Aid for Flood Victims," *Salt Lake Tribune,* August 16, 1923, 1.

21. "Cloudbursts Hit Utah," *Salt Lake Tribune,* July 11, 1930, 1; "Might Have Been Worse," *Salt Lake Tribune,* July 12, 1930, 6.

22. " 'Acres of Trees' Went Over Road, Eurekan Tells," *Salt Lake Tribune,* August 12, 1930, 8; " 'Best Land in Utah' Ruined, Blood Finds," *Salt Lake Tribune,* August 12, 1930, 1.

23. "Work Begun to Rebuild Flood Area," *Salt Lake Tribune,* August 14, 1930, 1; "Utah Counts Flood Toll; Maps Relief," *Salt Lake Tribune,* August 15, 1930, 1.

24. "3 Cloudbursts Hit Tintic; Flood Prevention Urged," *Deseret News,* August 14, 1930, 1; "Utah Counts Flood Toll; Maps Relief," *Salt Lake Tribune,* August 15, 1930, 1; "Writer Gives Reasons for Recent Floods," *Salt Lake Tribune,* August 18, 1930, 6; "Governor Lauded for Placing Blame," *Salt Lake Tribune,* August 22, 1930, 14.

25. "Section Checks on New Storm Damage," *Salt Lake Tribune,* September 6, 1930, 1.

26. Flood Commission of Utah, Report of the Commission, *Torrential Floods in Northern Utah, 1930* (Logan, Utah: Utah State Agricultural College, 1931), 7, 17.

27. U.S. Congress, Senate, Committee on Public Lands and Surveys, *Granting Remaining Unreserved Public Lands to States, Hearings . . . on S. 17, S. 2272, and S. 4060,* 72nd Cong., 1st sess., 1932.

28. Senator William H. King of Utah introduced a cession bill along with the Nye-Evans and Walsh bill, but showed little interest in politicking for its passage—no doubt acceding to the views of his constituency.

29. Gates, *History of Public Land Law Development,* 516.